How to Play Djen

West African Rhythms for Beginners

by Alan Dworsky and Betsy Sansby

Cover art by Toni Pawlowsky

Illustrations by Jay Kendell

DANCING HANDS MUSIC

How to Play Djembe – West African Rhythms for Beginners

Published by
Dancing Hands Music
4275 Churchill Circle
Minnetonka, MN 55345
phone or fax: 952-933-0781
dancinghands.com

Book design and production by MacLean & Tuminelly
Cover art by Toni Pawlowsky
Illustrations by Jay Kendell (phone 503-625-1121 in the Portland area)
except illustration on page 78 by Robert Jackson

CD recorded at Kurnow-Schnitzer Productions
Engineer: Bobby Schnitzer
Mastering by Doug Wild at Wild Audio

All parts on the CD performed by Sidi Mohamed "Joh" Camara
(phone 617-905-8376 in the Boston area)

Printed in the United States of America
with soy ink on recycled, acid-free paper by Banta ISG (Viking Press)

ISBN 0-9638801-4-4

We would like to express our gratitude to all our teachers, especially Joh Camara and all the teachers at the Jembe and Dance Institute in Greensboro, North Carolina. We are also indebted to the creators of all the sources listed at the back of this book and to all the unknown creators of the rhythms of West Africa.

Table of Contents

CHAPTER 1

How this book works

Did you walk into a drum store and walk out with a djembe? You're in good company. For centuries the djembe has been the driving force in the traditional music of West Africa. Now this light, powerful instrument – with its deep bass tones and explosive slaps – is fast becoming the hottest drum in the world.

This book is a complete, step-by-step course for beginners on how to play djembe. Right from the start you'll be learning interlocking parts for some of the most popular West African rhythms: Kuku, Djole, Kassa, Madan, Suku, Sunguru Bani, and Tiriba. After working through only a few lessons, you'll be able to put the parts together and start playing these irresistible rhythms with your friends.

While you learn the patterns, you'll also learn how to make each of the basic strokes – bass, tone, and slap – with proper playing technique. We use life-like illustrations to show how each stroke looks from the outside and give detailed descriptions to explain how each stroke feels from the inside.

The CD that comes with the book gives you a chance to hear how each part sounds separately and how the parts for each rhythm fit together. It was recorded by Joh Camara, a master drummer from Bamako, Mali. Each rhythm lasts at least five minutes, so you'll have plenty of time to play along. And when Joh solos during the final three minutes of each track, you'll feel the thrill of playing your part along with an ensemble and lead drummer.

The book is organized into thirteen lessons arranged roughly in order of difficulty. Within each lesson, the patterns start simple and gradually get more complex. But you'll hardly notice it, because we make sure you get the right-size steps, in the right order, at just the right time.

The charts are so simple you'll be able to understand them even if you've never read music before. We've also made them as big as possible so they're easy to read from a distance. And we don't just dump a pile of charts on you and leave. We'll be with you every step of the way, anticipating your questions, pointing out whatever is most important, and explaining whatever we think will make your journey easier.

We've done everything else we could to make this book as user-friendly as possible. Whenever we introduce a new Playing Principle or Practice Principle, we highlight it in the margin for easy reference. Whenever we introduce a new term, we print it in bold letters, define it on the spot, and toss it in the Glossary at the back of the book. We've included two pages of blank charts you can photocopy and use for writing down new patterns. And we've used a special binding that makes the book stay open and lie flat.

At the back of the book you'll find Sources for Further Study. You can use the instructional books and videos listed there to learn the bell and dundun parts that traditionally accompany the djembe parts you'll be learning here. And you can use the other sources to learn about the cultures and the contexts in which these rhythms are played in West Africa. Our hope is that by helping you learn to play the djembe, you'll be inspired to go beyond this book and join an ensemble, play for dance classes, go to drum camp, or study with a teacher who can give you what we cannot.

CHAPTER 2

Understanding the charts

Here's a sample chart:

PATTERN 1-7   CD TRACK 2, R CHANNEL

1	+	2	+	3	+	4	+	1	+	2	+	3	+	4	+
*				*				O		O		O	O		
R				L				R		L		R	L		

Box charts like these are the simplest charts for notating drum rhythms. Time moves from left to right and each vertical column shows what's happening on a single beat. Each of the three horizontal rows gives you a different kind of information.

The top row – or "count row" – tells you how to count a rhythm. The symbol "+" stands for "AND." The shaded boxes on the count row indicate the pulse, which we'll explain in Lesson 1.

The middle row tells you when and how to hit the drum. If there's a symbol in a box, you hit the drum on that beat with the stroke indicated by the symbol. For example, in the chart above, there's an asterisk in the box under beat 1. The asterisk is the symbol for the bass stroke, so you play a bass stroke on beat 1. If a box is empty, like the box under the AND of 1, you play nothing on that beat.

Here are all the symbols for how to hit the drum:

Bass tone	=	✳
Open tone	=	O
Slap	=	▲
Ghost stroke or touch	=	•
Open tone flam	=	°O

We use two additional symbols on the count row. Brackets – [ ] – indicate phrasing. An underlined symbol – <u>▲</u> – indicates where you should start playing. We explain more about these in Lesson 2.

The bottom row on the chart tells you which hand to use. You'll be using both hands on all the rhythms, but the right hand often plays a dominant role. If you're left-handed, you can reverse the hands.

To make the charts as big as possible, we've made them just long enough to show one or two repetitions of each pattern. But you should think of every chart as being written in a circle. When you get to the end, go back to the beginning and start over without missing a beat.

We haven't put any tempo markings on our charts. Ultimately, the tempo of a rhythm will depend on your playing situation. The important thing for now is to play each pattern at a steady tempo and not to leave a pattern until it grooves.

Think of every chart as being written in a circle. When you get to the end, go back to the beginning and start over without missing a beat.

This system of notation works great for teaching you the patterns in this book. But no system of written notation can capture the subtle nuances of a live rhythm. So while you're working your way through this book, be sure to listen to how the patterns are played on the CD.

CHAPTER 3

About the play-along CD

All the rhythms you'll be learning in this book have at least two djembe parts, and some have three. On the CD, you'll hear how each part sounds separately and how the parts for each rhythm fit together. You won't hear any of the simplified patterns or exercises we've included in the book. We left those out so you'd have plenty of time to play along with extended recordings of Kuku, Djole, Kassa, Madan, Suku, Sunguru Bani, and Tiriba.

All the djembe parts on the CD were recorded by Sidi Mohamed "Joh" Camara, a master drummer, dancer, and choreographer born in Bamako, Mali. Before moving to Boston in 1995, Joh was the chief choreographer of two of the most renowned West African dance companies: Troupe Mande and Troupe Sewa.

How to locate a part on the CD

Look above the chart. On the right you'll find the track number and channel where the part can be found:

PATTERN 1-7   CD TRACK 2, R CHANNEL

1	+	2	+	3	+	4	+	1	+	2	+	3	+	4	+
✳				✳				O		O		O	O		
R				L				R		L		R	L		

If you don't see a reference to the CD above a chart, it means the pattern is an exercise that isn't on the CD.

Look at the CD itself. On its face you'll find the track numbers and channels for each part.

How the parts are arranged on the CD

Two-part rhythms Each two-part rhythm is recorded on a single track. The first part is recorded on the right channel and the second part is recorded on the left. To hear the first part by itself, set the balance on your stereo all the way to the right. To hear the second part by itself, set the balance all the way to the left. To hear both parts together set the balance in the middle.

Three-part rhythms Each three-part rhythm is recorded on two tracks. The first track is recorded just like a two-part rhythm: first part on the right channel and second part on the left. The second track contains the third part by itself on the right channel and the first two parts together on the left. To hear all three parts together, set the balance on the second track in the middle.

Djembe solos The running time for each track is between five and six minutes. About two minutes into each track, Joh Camara adds a djembe solo, which is recorded on both channels. The solo is mixed quieter than it would be on a pure music CD so you can hear the support drum parts better.

How to work with the CD

You don't have to wait until Lesson 1 to start listening to the CD. Although it's designed to be instructional, it's also great for just listening. And the more familiar you are with the rhythms, the easier they'll be to play. So tear it out of its sleeve right now – if you haven't already – and pop it into your CD player. Put it on when you're riding in your car, doing the dishes, or going for a walk. The sooner you immerse yourself in these hypnotic West African rhythms, the better.

When you're learning a specific part, here are the steps we recommend for working with the CD:

1. Before you start playing the part, listen to it all by itself by adjusting the balance on your stereo all the way to the right or left. Stop when the solo starts.

2. Turn off the CD and practice the part on your own until you can play it comfortably up to tempo.

3. Turn the CD back on and play along with the part. When the solo starts, hit "repeat" on your CD player and go back to the beginning of the track.

4. When you feel really solid on a part, set the balance on your stereo in the middle and play the part while listening to the other part or parts.

Once you've learned *two* parts to a rhythm, you can play one part while listening to the other. If it's a three-part rhythm, you can play one part while listening to the other two.

Eventually you'll be able to keep playing your part even after Joh starts his solo. That's when the real fun begins.

CHAPTER 4

Playing Position

There are two ways to play djembe: standing up and sitting down. We recommend you play sitting down, at least at first. That way all your energy and focus can go into mastering the basic strokes and the rhythms. Playing standing up is a separate skill that takes time and practice to master.

To play sitting down, the first thing you need is a good chair. It should be sturdy enough to provide a solid foundation for you while you play. A typical kitchen chair will work, but if you're shorter or taller than average you may need to find a chair of a different height.

When you're sitting in the right chair, your thighs will be parallel to the floor when your feet are flat on the floor. Pick a chair without arms. They get in the way when you play. And make sure the chair is open in front. You'll need to slide the bottom of the djembe under the seat while you play.

Once you've got your chair, sit towards the front of it with the djembe resting on the floor between your legs. Now tilt the drum forward away from your body. The angle of the drumhead in relation to the floor should be somewhere between 10 and 45 degrees. Next, while holding the drum with your hands, reach out with one foot and slide the drum back towards you until the bottom is a few inches under your chair and the drumhead is between your knees and thighs.

Tilting the drum allows the sound to come out the bottom. The further you tilt it forward, the more sound comes out – especially the bass. Tilting the drum also brings your hands and arms into proper alignment with the drumhead so your wrists aren't cramped and your hands and arms can move freely.

PLAYING
PRINCIPLE

Play sitting down.

If you're playing on carpet, you may want to put a piece of plywood under the djembe so the carpet doesn't muffle the sound. On the other hand, if you need to play quietly, playing on carpet is a good idea.

To hold the djembe in its tilted position, wrap your legs around it, crossing one foot over the other:

Another way to hold the djembe in its tilted position is to keep your feet flat on the floor and steady the drum with your knees, thighs, and feet. Experiment until you find the angle where the drum almost balances by itself. That way you'll only have to use gentle pressure with your knees and thighs instead of having to grip the drum.

If you're playing for a long time, you may want to switch positions so your legs don't get tired or sore. You may also want to experiment with hybrid positions, such as one leg wrapped around the djembe and the other steadying it from the side. Do whatever works for you.

Once you're comfortable holding the djembe in a tilted position, place your hands on the drumhead as in the illustration. If you think of the drumhead as the face of an old-fashioned clock, your right hand should be between the 4 and 5 and your left hand between the 7 and 8. Keep your hands in line with your forearms, so that you could draw a straight line from your elbow through your middle finger. Consider this hand position home base.

Now look closely at the drumhead. If there's a line across the middle, that's the spine of the goatskin. Turn the drum so that this line points straight at you. This is usually the best position for getting an even sound in both hands. If there are irregularities around the edge of your drumhead that might hurt your hands, try rotating the drum 180 degrees.

Before you start playing, take off any rings you're wearing. These can hurt your hands and damage the drumhead. You should also take off your watch or any bracelets that might rattle while you play or touch the drumhead. If the cuff of your shirt is loose, roll it up and make sure it stays out of the way.

Finally, check your posture. Your spine should be straight, you should be leaning slightly forward from the waist, and your elbows should be hanging loosely at your sides.

You're ready to play now, so let's get started.

CHAPTER 5

West African rhythms in four and the basic strokes

lesson

Kuku part 1, the bass, and the tone

Three basic strokes give the djembe its distinctive sound: the bass, the tone, and the slap. In this lesson, you'll learn the first two, starting with the bass. Making a bass stroke is one of the great pleasures of playing the djembe. Its deep thud resonates like an amplified heartbeat.

The deep thud of a bass stroke resonates like an amplified heartbeat.

To make a bass stroke, move your hand up and forward from the home base position toward the center of the drum, along the imaginary line running through your forearm and middle finger. Then simply bring it down onto the center of the drum and let it bounce up. Keep your fingers relaxed and together. Your thumb can be either pulled in against your index finger or extended away from your hand:

✳ = bass stroke

Most of the sound of the bass tone comes from your palm, so that's where you should focus the weight of your hand. You can also let your fingers make contact with the drumhead by keeping your whole hand flat, or you can lift your fingers slightly so only the palm makes contact. Experiment to see what sounds and feels best to you.

Once you feel comfortable playing bass strokes with either hand, you're ready to play them in time. Start by counting out loud "1 AND 2 AND 3 AND 4 AND." Then keep counting and play bass strokes on beats 1 and 3 with alternating hands. Remember to think of this chart – and every chart – as being written in a circle. When you get to the end, go right back to the beginning and start over without missing a beat:

PATTERN 1-1

1	+	2	+	3	+	4	+	1	+	2	+	3	+	4	+
✱				✱				✱				✱			
R				L				R				L			

You've just played the pulse in four. The **pulse** is the underlying metronomic rhythm people feel in their bodies when music is played. When you tap your foot to music, chances are you're tapping along with the pulse. When you dance, chances are you're moving your feet to the pulse.

African rhythms are all organized around a pulse. So whenever you drum, you need to know where the pulse is and how your part relates to it. In four, the way we're counting, the pulse in on 1 and 3 in each measure. That's why we shade those boxes on the count row.

It's a good idea to get in the habit of keeping a pulse going in your body while you play. One way is to tap your foot. If you're holding the djembe with your feet crossed, you can tap the outside edge of the top foot. If you're sitting with your legs on either side of the djembe, you can tap the toe or heel of one foot. If tapping your foot while you hold the djembe doesn't work, find somewhere else in your body to keep the pulse going: nod your head, move your shoulders, rock your midsection or your pelvis. The idea is to express your internal awareness of the pulse as an external body movement.

Musical time-out: Counting in four

When we say a pattern is in **four**, we mean it can be notated on a chart with four pulses and four subdivisions – or **beats** – to each pulse. Our charts in four are divided into two measures of eighth-note beats. The pulse falls on beats 1 and 3 in each measure. This way of counting is called **cut-time**:

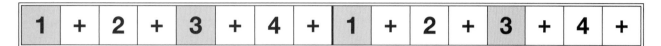

We could have counted patterns in four in **4/4 time**. In 4/4, a measure is divided into four quarter notes, and each quarter note is divided into four sixteenth notes. This way of counting has the advantage of putting the pulse on each numbered beat:

We've chosen to chart in cut-time rather than 4/4 for several reasons. We find it's easier to work with two short 8-beat measures than with one long 16-beat measure. This is especially true with the patterns in four in this book, because most of them are 8-beat patterns. We also like the counting system in cut-time better because it gives you a number as a reference point every two beats instead of every four. And we find it easier and more natural to talk about rhythms in cut-time. We'd feel silly talking about the "ee" of 3 or the "uh" of 4.

If you're used to counting in 4/4 and don't want to change, you don't have to. Just think of each eighth note on our charts as a sixteenth note instead. This won't change the sound or the speed of the patterns. And to help you out, in each lesson we've included a chart in 4/4 for whatever part is the subject of the lesson.

Now let's get back to bass strokes. Earlier we said you could keep your thumb extended away from your hand when you make a bass stroke. This works fine on single strokes. But when you want to play a series of fast bass strokes with alternating hands – as you'll do in the next exercise – you'll need to pull your thumbs in to make room for both hands on the drumhead. Try to make the strokes sound the same in both hands:

PATTERN 1-2

1	+	2	+	3	+	4	+	1	+	2	+	3	+	4	+
✳	✳	✳	✳	✳	✳	✳	✳	✳	✳	✳	✳	✳	✳	✳	✳
R	L	R	L	R	L	R	L	R	L	R	L	R	L	R	L

Now you're ready to learn your second stroke: the open tone or "tone" for short. Of the three basic strokes, the open tone is in the middle register between the bass on the low end and the slap on top. Depending on the drum, the tone can sound dry and muted or round and bright.

When you make an open tone, the alignment of your hand in relation to the edge of the drumhead is critical. Your hand should make contact with the edge of the drumhead at the crease where your fingers join the palm:

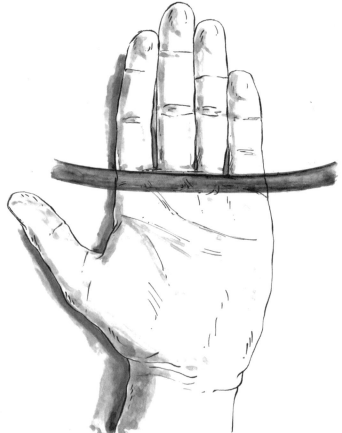

The easiest way to get the feel of the open tone stroke is to pretend you're dribbling a basketball. Raise your fingers a few inches off the drum by flexing your wrist and lifting your forearm slightly. Keep your fingers relaxed and together or slightly apart, and keep your thumb extended away from your hand so you don't whack it on the edge of the drum.

Now bring your hand down and bounce your fingers off the drumhead. The part of your palm just below the crease where your fingers join the hand should make only light contact with the edge of the drum. Don't let your fingers linger on the drumhead or you'll muffle the tone:

O = open tone

Now that you understand the basic hand-position and motion required to make an open tone, we want to focus on some details about the stroke that you can't pick up by watching someone play. When you make an open tone, your fingers should make contact with the drumhead between the crease where the fingers join the palm and the last knuckle of each finger. The pads of your fingertips – the fingerprint zone – should touch the drumhead just barely or not at all. And the weight of your hand should be focused as much as possible on the bony joint at the first knuckle away from the palm:

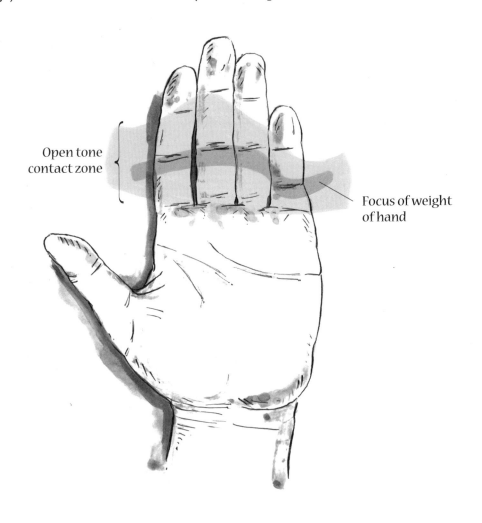

Open tone contact zone

Focus of weight of hand

Once you've played an open tone, if you don't need to make another stroke immediately with the same hand, you can let your wrist drop and leave your hand resting on the edge of the drum. You can also let your thumb drop down below the edge of the drum if you want. Just make sure your fingers are up so they don't muffle the head.

Now play open tones on the pulse with alternating hands:

PATTERN 1-3

1	+	2	+	3	+	4	+	1	+	2	+	3	+	4	+
O				O				O				O			
R				L				R				L			

Next put an open tone on every beat. Just as you did with the bass strokes, try to make them sound the same in both hands:

PATTERN 1-4

1	+	2	+	3	+	4	+	1	+	2	+	3	+	4	+
O	O	O	O	O	O	O	O	O	O	O	O	O	O	O	O
R	L	R	L	R	L	R	L	R	L	R	L	R	L	R	L

Now that you know two strokes, you're ready to switch back and forth between them. In the next pattern, you'll play bass tones in the first measure and open tones in the second:

PATTERN 1-5

1	+	2	+	3	+	4	+	1	+	2	+	3	+	4	+
✳				✳				O				O			
R				L				R				L			

Everything's the same in the next pattern except we've added a tone on 2 in the second measure. This changes the hand pattern in the second measure from RL to RLR:

PATTERN 1-6

1	+	2	+	3	+	4	+	1	+	2	+	3	+	4	+
✳				✳				O		O		O			
R				L				R		L		R			

When you add one more tone on the AND of 3 in the second measure, you'll be playing the first part from Kuku, a celebration rhythm from Guinea. Because this part only has bass strokes and open tones, it's usually played on a djembe with a low voice.

Before you try playing this part, get out your CD and listen to it first. Put on track 2 with the balance on your stereo adjusted all the way to the right. The first thing you'll hear on this track – and every track – is the **break**, a brief introductory phrase that sets the tempo. We don't teach you how to play this break until Lesson 9, but here's a chart of it so you can see what it looks like. Notice it ends on 3 in the second measure:

1	+	2	+	3	+	4	+	1	+	2	+	3	+	4	+
°O		O	O		O			O	O	△	△	△			

After the break the part will begin on ONE – the first beat in the first measure. Once you've listened to the part, turn off the CD and practice the part on your own. Counting out loud while you play will help you keep steady time:

PATTERN 1-7   **CD TRACK 2, R CHANNEL**

1	+	2	+	3	+	4	+	1	+	2	+	3	+	4	+
✳				✳				O		O		O	O		
R				L				R		L		R	L		

Here's how the same pattern looks counted in 4/4:

PATTERN 1-7 (IN 4/4)   **CD TRACK 2, R CHANNEL**

1	e	+	a	2	e	+	a	3	e	+	a	4	e	+	a
✳				✳				O		O		O	O		
R				L				R		L		R	L		

Once you can play this part up to tempo, turn on the CD again and play along with the part all by itself.

Congratulations. You've just learned your first authentic West African djembe part. This part – and all the parts you'll be learning – are called **support drum parts** because they provide the rhythmic foundation for the dancers and the lead djembe player. You'll learn the second support drum part from Kuku in the next lesson.

Kuku part 2, the slap, and phrasing

The second part from Kuku is one of the most popular djembe patterns played in America. We've called it the "second" part only because we've chosen to teach it second, not because it's less important than the "first" part or more important than the "third" part we teach in the next lesson. In Africa, a number of factors determine how many and which parts of a rhythm are played, including the number of drummers available, their level of experience, the tempo, what other parts are being played, and the preferences of the lead drummer.

In the last lesson you learned how to make two of the three basic strokes: the bass and the tone. To play the second part from Kuku you need to know how to make the third basic stroke: the slap. So that's where we're going to start.

The slap has a sharp sound like the crack of a whip. It's made by bringing the pads of your fingertips down in a whip-like motion onto the drumhead. As with the open tone, the relation of your palm to the edge of the drum is critical. Many master drummers make the slap and the open tone without changing the alignment of their hands in relation to the edge of the drum by making subtle adjustments in their wrists and fingers.

But many players – especially beginners – find it easier to move the hand slightly forward toward the center of the drum to make the slap. This means the point of contact with the edge of the drum when you make a slap will be a couple inches lower on your palm than when you make an open tone:

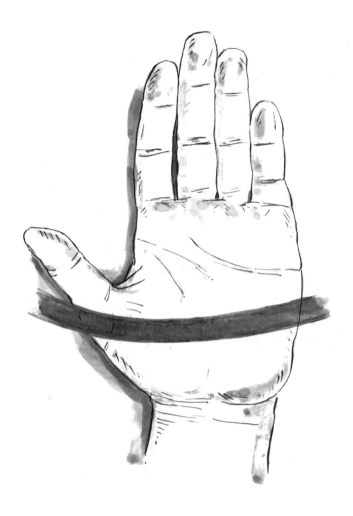

To get ready to make the slap, lift your hand an inch or two off the drum by raising your forearm slightly. At the same time, flex your wrist and pull your fingers up until your hand makes at least a 45 degree angle with the drumhead. Keep your fingers relaxed and together or slightly apart. Your thumb should be away from your hand, but it can be closer than it was when you made the open tone, especially if it stays above the edge of the drum throughout the stroke.

When you bring your hand down, only the pad of each fingertip – the fingerprint section – will make contact with the drumhead:

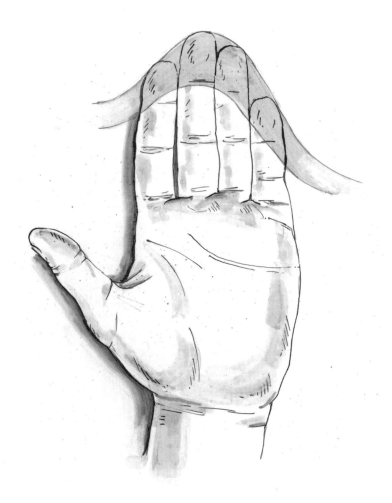

This will happen naturally if the point of contact between your palm and the edge of the drum is on the lower half of your palm, as indicated in the illustration on the previous page. To see this for yourself, rest your palm on the edge of the drum with your fingers raised and relaxed and slightly curved. Now just let them fall to the drumhead. Your fingers will naturally make contact with the drumhead only at the pads. Do this little experiment a few times with both hands to get the feel of the slap motion.

Now you're ready to try the slap stroke. Bring your hand up by raising your forearm and flexing your wrist. Now bring it down in a whip-like motion and bounce the pads of your fingertips off the drumhead as if it were redhot. It may help to imagine that you've got a lead weight in each fingertip and that the rest of each finger is completely weightless. Your palm should make only light contact with the edge of the drum:

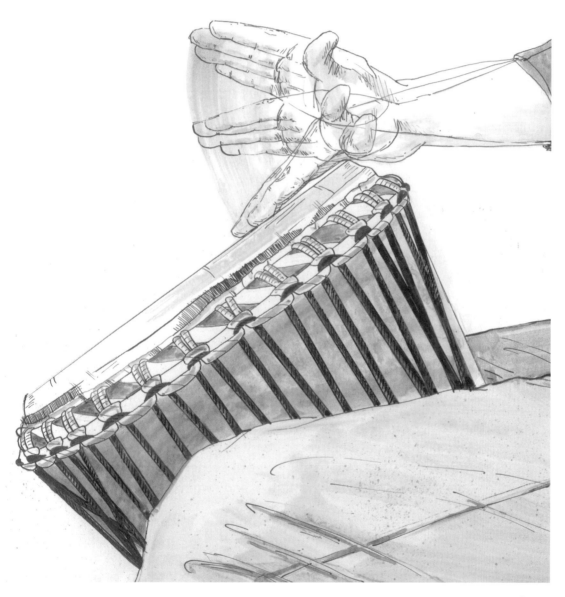

$\triangle$ = slap

Once you've played a slap, if you don't need to make another stroke immediately with the same hand, you can let your wrist drop and leave your palm resting on the edge of the drum – just as you can with the open tone. Again, make sure your fingers are up so you don't muffle the head.

PLAYING
PRINCIPLE

The sound of the
slap comes not
from sheer force
but from a relaxed
snap of the wrist.

Of the three basic strokes, the slap is the most difficult to master. Even though it makes the loudest sound on the djembe, it requires the most subtle technique. The most common mistake made by beginners is whacking the drum too hard in an effort to get a good slap. The important thing to remember is that the sound of a slap comes not from sheer force but from a relaxed snap of the wrist.

PLAYING
PRINCIPLE

Only play as loud
as you can play
comfortably.

So go easy at first. If your hands hurt, you're doing something wrong. Only play as loud as you can play comfortably. As your technique improves, you'll be able to play louder with less effort.

Now play slaps on the pulse with alternating hands:

PATTERN 2-1

1	+	2	+	3	+	4	+	1	+	2	+	3	+	4	+
△				△				△				△			
R				L				R				L			

You can turn this simple pattern into an exercise in self-awareness by paying attention to each slap you make. When you get a slap that sounds good and feels comfortable, stop and analyze what you just did. Ask yourself: "What was different that time?" "What made that one better than the rest?" You might find that you get a better sound by centering the force of the slap on a particular finger or fingers. Or you might get a better sound by striking with the outside of your fingertips rather than the fingerprint section. Since everyone's hands are different, ultimately your own body will be your best teacher.

Since everyone's hands are different, ultimately your own body will be your best teacher.

Now play a series of faster slaps with alternating hands. Remember to go easy:

PATTERN 2-2

1	+	2	+	3	+	4	+	1	+	2	+	3	+	4	+
Δ	Δ	Δ	Δ	Δ	Δ	Δ	Δ	Δ	Δ	Δ	Δ	Δ	Δ	Δ	Δ
R	L	R	L	R	L	R	L	R	L	R	L	R	L	R	L

The next exercise will help you get ready to play the second part from Kuku. It'll also give you practice switching between slaps and tones. Try to make the two sounds as distinct as possible by focusing on your technique:

PATTERN 2-3

1	+	2	+	3	+	4	+	1	+	2	+	3	+	4	+
Δ	Δ	O	O	O	O	Δ		Δ	Δ	O	O	O	O	Δ	
R	L	R	L	R	L	R		R	L	R	L	R	L	R	

In the next chart, we've taken out the first two slaps in each measure and put a bass stroke in the left hand on 1. Notice we've underlined the slap on 4 in the second measure. That means you should start playing the pattern there. If you don't see any symbol underlined on a chart, it means you start playing on ONE.

△ = Whenever a symbol is underlined, it means you start playing there.

To play this pattern, start counting from ONE and then come in when you get to 4 in the second measure. Then go back to the beginning of the chart and continue on from there. Make sure you feel the bass in the left hand as the pulse. If it helps, continue to count out loud while you play:

PATTERN 2-4

1	+	2	+	3	+	4	+	1	+	2	+	3	+	4	+
✳		O	O	O	O	△		✳		O	O	O	O	△	
L		R	L	R	L	R		L		R	L	R	L	R	

PRACTICE PRINCIPLE

Count out loud while you play each new pattern.

It's a good idea to count out loud while you play any new pattern. But counting is like the scaffolding around a new building. Once the building is finished, the scaffolding comes down. Once you know the rhythm of a new pattern, stop counting and just feel it.

Once you know the rhythm of a new pattern, stop counting and just feel it.

The next pattern is the same as the last except we've taken out the tone on the AND of 3 in each measure. Remember to start on 4 in the second measure:

PATTERN 2-5

1	+	2	+	3	+	4	+	1	+	2	+	3	+	4	+
✳		O	O	O		△		✳		O	O	O		△	
L		R	L	R		R		L		R	L	R		R	

Now you're ready to play the second part from Kuku. It's a thinned-out version of the pattern you just played. All you need to do is take out the tone on 3 in each measure. You can hear the part by itself on the left channel of track 2. First you'll hear the break – which ends on 3 in the second measure – and then the part will start on 4:

PATTERN 2-6   **CD TRACK 2, L CHANNEL**

1	+	2	+	3	+	4	+	1	+	2	+	3	+	4	+
✳		O	O			Δ		✳		O	O			Δ	
L		R	L			R		L		R	L			R	

As you listen to this part on the CD, you may notice subtleties in the timing that aren't notated on the chart. When Kuku is played fast, which it usually is, the timing gets straighter.

Here's the same part charted in 4/4:

PATTERN 2-6 (IN 4/4)   **CD TRACK 2, L CHANNEL**

1	e	+	a	2	e	+	a	3	e	+	a	4	e	+	a
✳		O	O			Δ		✳		O	O			Δ	
L		R	L			R		L		R	L			R	

Before we go further, let's review what you know about this part so far. You know the rhythmic pattern. You know how it fits with the pulse. And you know how to come in after the break. There's just one more thing you need to know: the phrasing.

Phrasing refers to where you perceive the beginning and end of a repeating pattern. To understand this concept, it's helpful to think of a rhythmic phrase like a sentence. Even if you repeat a sentence over and over, you always know where it begins and ends. For example, no matter how many times you repeat the sentence, "Let's have some fun," you never lose your awareness that each repetition begins with "Let's" and ends with "fun." And that awareness affects how you say the sentence every time.

While we were recording the CD with Joh Camara, we discussed the concept of phrasing with him. Joh explained that he has a definite sense of where each part he plays begins and ends. He then clarified the phrasing of each part you'll be learning in this book, and this is the phrasing we'll be teaching you. We don't mean to imply that all other phrasings are wrong. Drummers from other West African countries or regions may perceive the phrasing of the same patterns differently.

What's important to understand is that how you perceive the phrasing of a part will influence how you play it. And knowing Joh's phrasing of each part in this book will help you play with the subtle nuances of emphasis and timing you hear on the CD.

Brackets – [ ] – indicate phrasing.

For this part from Kuku, the phrase starts on 2 in each measure and ends on 1. In the next chart, we've used brackets to indicate this phrasing.

Don't play anything for now. Just look at the chart:

PATTERN 2-6   CD TRACK 2, L CHANNEL

1	+	2	+	3	+	4	+	1	+	2	+	3	+	4	+
✳]		[O	O			◬		✳]		[O	O			◬	
L		R	L			R		L		R	L			R	

You're probably wondering why you start playing on 4 if the phrase actually starts on 2. Good question. According to Joh, you do this to bridge the gap between the end of the break and the beginning of the phrase.

To remember the phrasing of a part, it often helps to come up with a sentence that matches the rhythmic phrase. For this part from Kuku, we use the same sentence we used in the example above: "Let's have some fun." Saying it while you play the part will help you hang on to the phrasing.

We've put this sentence on the chart below. Each word is underneath the stroke it corresponds with. We put "FUN" in caps because it falls on the pulse. Even though you start playing on 4 in the second measure, remember that the first slap and bass you play are a *fragment* of the phrase. It's like saying the sentence fragment "some FUN" before launching into the full sentence – "some FUN, Let's have some FUN, Let's have some FUN ...":

1	+	2	+	3	+	4	+	1	+	2	+	3	+	4	+
*]		[O	O			△		*]		[O	O			△	
FUN.		Let's	have			some		FUN.		Let's	have			some	

Understanding the phrasing of this part will also help you understand how it fits with other parts. Here's a chart with the first two parts from Kuku. We've used brackets to indicate the phrasing of both parts. Notice that the first part is one long phrase and the second is two shorter phrases. Also notice what happens on ONE – the second phrase ends where the first phrase begins:

1	+	2	+	3	+	4	+	1	+	2	+	3	+	4	+	
*]		[O	O			△		*]		[O	O			△		Part 2
[*				*				O		O		O	O]			Part 1

Now that you know two parts from Kuku, it's time to get together with a friend, eat some good food, light some candles, and put the parts together. If you don't have someone to play with, eat the food, light the candles, set the balance on your stereo in the middle, and play along with the CD. Enjoy!

Kuku part 3 and playing with a group

In this lesson, you'll learn the third part from Kuku. The following exercise will help you get ready for it. It's just tones in the left hand and slaps in the right. The tones fall on each pulse and the slaps fall on the beat before. To make sure you get the timing right, count out loud while you play:

PATTERN 3-1

1	+	2	+	3	+	4	+	1	+	2	+	3	+	4	+
O			Δ	O			Δ	O			Δ	O			Δ
L			R	L			R	L			R	L			R

PRACTICE PRINCIPLE

Play along with a metronome.

If you've got a metronome, you can test yourself by playing along with it. African rhythms are generally played at a steady tempo, and practicing with a metronome will help you develop steady time. On this pattern, make sure the click of the metronome coincides with each pulse in your left hand.

The next exercise is a variation of the last one. We've kept the slap-tone pair on the AND of 2 and beat 3 in each measure and replaced the other slap-tone pair with two tones on 1 and the AND of 1:

PATTERN 3-2

1	+	2	+	3	+	4	+	1	+	2	+	3	+	4	+
O	O		Δ	O				O	O		Δ	O			
R	L		R	L				R	L		R	L			

When you add a tone on the AND of 3 and a slap on 4 in each measure, you've got the third part from Kuku. You can hear this part on the right channel of track 3 on the CD. After the break, the part starts on ONE:

PATTERN 3-3   CD TRACK 3, R CHANNEL

1	+	2	+	3	+	4	+	1	+	2	+	3	+	4	+
O	O			∆	O	O	∆		O	O		∆	O	O	∆
R	L			R	L	R	L		R	L		R	L	R	L

PATTERN 3-3 (IN 4/4)   CD TRACK 3, R CHANNEL

1	e	+	a	2	e	+	a	3	e	+	a	4	e	+	a
O	O			∆	O	O	∆		O	O		∆	O	O	∆
R	L			R	L	R	L		R	L		R	L	R	L

Now for the phrasing. This is another pattern where the first note you play is *different* from the start of the phrase. Although you start playing this part on ONE, the repeating phrase actually starts on the AND of 2. To help you feel the phrasing, say the sentence "I wanna play djembe" while you play:

PLAYING PRINCIPLE

Where you start playing a pattern and where the phrase starts are often two different places.

PATTERN 3-3   CD TRACK 3, R CHANNEL

1	+	2	+	3	+	4	+	1	+	2	+	3	+	4	+
O	O]			[∆	O	O	∆		O	O]		[∆	O	O	∆
DJEM-	be.			I	WAN-	na	play		DJEM-	be.		I	WAN-	na	play

Notice that the first time you play the two tones on 1 and the AND of 1 you're just playing a fragment of the phrase. This fragment bridges the gap between the end of the break and the start of the phrase on the AND of 2.

The next chart shows you how all three parts from Kuku fit together. Notice that the first part has six strokes, the second has eight, and the third has twelve. The more strokes a part has, the more stamina you're going to need to play it, so choose the part that fits your level of endurance. Also notice that whoever plays the second part will be the first to start playing. The other two parts start on ONE:

PATTERN 1-7, 2-6, & 3-3   **CD TRACK 3, R & L CHANNELS**

	1	+	2	+	3	+	4	+	1	+	2	+	3	+	4	+
Part 3	O	O]		[Δ	O	O	Δ		O	O]		[Δ	O	O	Δ	
Part 2	*]		[O	O			Δ		*]		[O	O			Δ	
Part 1	[*				*				O		O		O	O]		

Playing alone can be a joyful experience, but nothing beats playing with a group. That's how these rhythms were meant to be played. In Africa, every important event in the life of a community – from weddings to funerals and from planting to harvesting – is an occasion for people of all ages to join together in drumming, dance, and song. Once you've experienced the thrill of drumming with a group – weaving your part into a larger tapestry of sound, participating in a community created and connected by something deeper than words – you'll be hooked.

If at first you can't find a group, at least try to find a partner to play with. You'll learn twice as fast and have more than twice the fun. Just knowing your partner is counting on you will help you keep to a regular practice schedule. When you get stuck, you'll have someone there to pull you out; when the rhythms are flowing, you'll have someone there to celebrate with.

Whenever you do get a chance to play with a group, there are a few things you need to watch out for. For example, when you play alone, you can stop whenever you like. But when you play with a group, there's an expectation that you'll continue playing your part for as long as a rhythm is played. If you're lucky enough to be asked to play for a

West African dance class, you may be expected to play the same rhythm for an hour or more. This means if your neck gets sore, or sweat starts to run into your eyes, or a fly lands on your nose, you keep playing.

When you're playing with a group, if your neck gets sore, or sweat starts to run into your eyes, or a fly lands on your nose, keep playing.

When you play alone you can close your eyes and turn inward. But when you play with a group, you need to keep your eyes open to stay connected and to watch for signals from others. You may get a distress signal from someone who's lost or unsolicited help from someone who's noticed that you are. If the group has a leader, you may get a signal to change the tempo or volume.

PLAYING PRINCIPLE

Keep your eyes open when you play with others.

And speaking of volume, once you start playing with a group, you need to pay attention to volume – especially when you play indoors – to make sure you don't damage your hearing. Volume isn't an issue in West Africa, where the djembe is traditionally played outside. But when you play indoors the sound has nowhere to go. Instead of dissipating out into the atmosphere it reverberates off the walls and comes back to bombard your eardrums. If your ears ring after you've been drumming, the music was too loud. And over time, loud music will damage your hearing.

PLAYING PRINCIPLE

Pay attention to volume – especially when you play indoors – to make sure you don't damage your hearing.

If you know you're going to be playing loud music indoors, there are two things you can do to protect your ears. First, choose your seat carefully. Don't sit with your head a few inches in front of a bell or giant dun-dun. Second, get yourself a pair of earplugs. You can get a cheap pair at a drugstore, but they tend to distort the sound. You're better off getting a custom-fitted pair from an audiologist. They cost about a hundred dollars and they dampen all frequencies evenly. Whatever you do, don't risk damaging your hearing. Hearing loss is sometimes painful and always permanent.

PLAYING PRINCIPLE

Choose your seat carefully when you play with a group.

You also need to protect your hands when you play with a group. A lot of beginners hurt their hands trying to hear themselves play. Instead of playing louder and louder, focus on the feel of the strokes you're making. The vibration in your fingertips will tell you when you've made a good slap.

Djole part 1 and maximizing speed and efficiency

In this lesson you're going to learn the first part from Djole (jo-lay), a rhythm from Sierra Leone that has been adapted in Guinea as a celebration rhythm. The timing of the part is easy but it's an athletic pattern that requires skill and stamina. Start by alternating between two basses and two tones. This exercise will give you practice moving your hands forward and backward on the drumhead – a skill you'll need for the first part from Djole:

PATTERN 4-1

1	+	2	+	3	+	4	+	1	+	2	+	3	+	4	+
✳	✳	O	O	✳	✳	O	O	✳	✳	O	O	✳	✳	O	O
R	L	R	L	R	L	R	L	R	L	R	L	R	L	R	L

PLAYING PRINCIPLE

To maximize speed and efficiency, play bass strokes close to the edge of the drumhead.

PLAYING PRINCIPLE

To maximize speed and efficiency, keep your hands close to the drumhead.

The faster you play this pattern, the smaller your hand and arm movements need to be. One way to maximize your speed and efficiency is to play your bass strokes close to the edge of the drumhead. This means your palm will land in the open tone zone, minimizing the forward and backward motion of the arm.

You can also maximize speed and efficiency on *all* your strokes by minimizing the up-and-down motion of your arms. Keep your hands low – as close to the drumhead as possible. Experienced drummers sometimes do raise their hands high in the air when they play a solo to play louder or to create a dramatic effect. But extra arm motion can compromise speed and accuracy, and – especially with a beginner – can lead to injury. So play close, at least for now.

In the next chart, we've taken out the second bass stroke in each pair. This thinning of the original pattern creates a repeating three-note phrase – a pair of tones leading to a bass stroke on each pulse. Notice that you start playing on 4 in the second measure. Count out loud while you're learning the pattern:

PATTERN 4-2

1	+	2	+	3	+	4	+	1	+	2	+	3	+	4	+
✳		O	O	✳		O	O	✳		O	O	✳		O̲	O
R		R	L	R		R	L	R		R	L	R		R	L

Once you can feel the rhythm of this pattern without counting, reinforce the phrasing by saying "To the PULSE" while you play each threenote phrase:

PATTERN 4-3

1	+	2	+	3	+	4	+	1	+	2	+	3	+	4	+
✳		O	O	✳		O	O	✳		O	O	✳		O̲	O
PULSE		To	the	PULSE		To	the	PULSE		To	the	PULSE		To	the

Now go back to the first exercise you did in this lesson and substitute slaps for tones. The trickiest part is playing the slaps on the way *back* from playing the bass strokes. Go slowly at first:

PATTERN 4-4

1	+	2	+	3	+	4	+	1	+	2	+	3	+	4	+
✳	✳	△	△	✳	✳	△	△	✳	✳	△	△	✳	✳	△	△
R	L	R	L	R	L	R	L	R	L	R	L	R	L	R	L

Next take out the second bass stroke in each pair, just as you did when you played this pattern with open tones. Notice that again the pattern

starts on 4 in the second measure. And remember the phrasing –
"To the PULSE, To the PULSE":

PATTERN 4-5

1	+	2	+	3	+	4	+	1	+	2	+	3	+	4	+
✳		△	△	✳		△	△	✳		△	△	✳		<u>△</u>	△
R		R	L	R		R	L	R		R	L	R		R	L

PRACTICE
PRINCIPLE

Play every new
pattern slowly
at first.

When you alternate between pairs of tones and pairs of slaps, you'll be playing the first part from Djole. The phrase starts where the part starts – with the tone on 4 in the second measure. To make sure your tones and slaps are clearly distinguishable from each other, start slow and take your time. In fact, it's a good idea to play every new pattern slowly at first. Strive for accuracy over speed, control over power.

Strive for accuracy over speed, control over power.

Speed and power will come naturally over time:

PATTERN 4-6   **CD TRACK 4, R CHANNEL**

1	+	2	+	3	+	4	+	1	+	2	+	3	+	4	+
✳		△	△	✳]		[O	O	✳		△	△	✳]		[<u>O</u>	O
R		R	L	R		R	L	R		R	L	R		R	L

PATTERN 4-6 (IN 4/4)   **CD TRACK 4, R CHANNEL**

1	e	+	a	2	e	+	a	3	e	+	a	4	e	+	a
✳		△	△	✳]		[O	O	✳		△	△	✳]		[<u>O</u>	O
R		R	L	R		R	L	R		R	L	R		R	L

We hope by now you've settled into some kind of regular practice routine. Here are some tips for making sure your practice sessions are pleasurable as well as productive.

The first thing to think about is your practice space. Find a place that's comfortable and inviting where you can make a lot of noise. Then clean it up. Get rid of the clutter. Make it beautiful, so you'll want to spend time there.

If possible, set aside a regular time to practice. Make it a ritual. If you have the flexibility in your schedule, pick the time of day when your energy is good and your hands feel the best.

Make practicing a ritual.

When it's practice time, change into comfortable clothes. Do what you can to protect yourself from distractions, like the phone, roommates, kids. Then take a minute to settle in. Stretch. Breathe. Focus.

Begin each practice session with a warm-up. Play gently at first, starting with bass strokes and tones before adding slaps. Feel your way into the drum.

Once you've limbered up, then start working on your lesson. If you find yourself stumbling when you try to play a pattern fast, go back to playing it slow. If one part of a pattern is tripping you up, isolate it and practice it separately. If you're still having trouble, put your hands in your lap, close your eyes, and visualize yourself playing the pattern correctly. If that doesn't work, try practicing something else or take a break. Come back to the pattern when you're fresh.

PRACTICE PRINCIPLE

Isolate difficult parts of a pattern and practice them separately.

Whatever you do, don't grind in mistakes. Playing a pattern incorrectly over and over only teaches your body to play it incorrectly. And don't beat yourself up either. Everybody makes mistakes. The key is knowing how not to repeat them.

PRACTICE PRINCIPLE

Don't grind in mistakes.

Once you can play a pattern correctly, shift your focus to technique. Really listen to yourself play. The tones should be clear and the slaps crisp, even when you play fast. And your strokes should sound the same in both hands. If there's a difference, analyze what your strong

PRACTICE PRINCIPLE

Let your strong hand teach your weak hand how to play.

hand is doing and mimic it in the other hand. Let your strong hand teach your weak hand how to play.

It's a good idea to include some review every time you practice. Reviewing reminds you that you're competent and you'll discover something new in these rhythms every time you play them.

Whenever you have a long practice session, take breaks to stretch and refresh yourself. Quit while you still have energy and end on a high note.

Djole part 2 and vocalizing a rhythm

The patterns you've played so far – except the first part from Kuku – have been one-measure patterns that repeat twice on a two-measure chart. The part for Djole you'll be learning in this lesson is a *two-measure* pattern that repeats only once on a two-measure chart.

To make it easier for you to learn this longer pattern, we're going to break it in half. You'll learn each half separately and then put the two together. This technique can be useful in learning almost any new pattern.

PRACTICE PRINCIPLE

Learn a new pattern a piece at a time.

Here's the first half of the pattern repeated twice. Remember to count out loud while you're learning it:

PATTERN 5-1

1	+	2	+	3	+	4	+	1	+	2	+	3	+	4	+
Δ		Δ	Δ		Δ	O	O	Δ		Δ	Δ		Δ	O	O
R			L	R		L	R	L	R		L	R		L	R	L

Another way to practice this – or any – pattern is to vocalize it using nonsense syllables. Vocalizing is a great way to learn and memorize a new pattern because you don't have to think about technique.

This method for learning and memorizing rhythms has been used around the world for centuries. In Indian music, for example, there's a highly developed system for vocalizing rhythms. A student may vocalize for a year or more before being allowed to touch a drum.

In the United States, the Nigerian Babatunde Olatunji has popularized a method of vocalizing in which each syllable tells you the kind of stroke and the hand that plays it: "pa" is a slap with the right hand, "ta" is a slap with the left, "go" is a tone with the right hand, "do" is a tone with the left, "goon" is a bass with the right hand, and "doon" is a bass with the left.

Many drummers develop their own style of vocalizing to learn parts and communicate with other drummers. For example, you could vocalize this pattern from Djole by saying "ta, ta-ta, ta-ti-ti" or "da, ka-da, ka-doo-doo" in time. If you wanted to teach the pattern to someone else, you could slow it down and use the names of the strokes instead of nonsense syllables: "slap, slap-slap, slap-tone-tone." There's no "correct" way to vocalize rhythms; the main point is to find a way that works for you. Remember: If you can say it, you can play it:

If you can say it, you can play it.

Here's the second half of the first part from Djole. All that's changed is that the slap on the AND of 2 in each measure has moved to beat 3:

PATTERN 5-2

1	+	2	+	3	+	4	+	1	+	2	+	3	+	4	+
Δ		Δ		Δ	Δ	O	O	Δ		Δ		Δ	Δ	O	O
R		L		R	L	R	L	R		L		R	L	R	L

Now you're ready to combine one measure from each of the last two patterns to create the full two-measure part. The part and the phrase start on ONE:

PATTERN 5-3   CD TRACK 4, L CHANNEL

1	+	2	+	3	+	4	+	1	+	2	+	3	+	4	+
[Δ		Δ	Δ		Δ	O	O	Δ		Δ		Δ	Δ	O	O]
R		L	R		L	R	L	R		L		R	L	R	L

PATTERN 5-3 (IN 4/4)   CD TRACK 4, L CHANNEL

1	e	+	a	2	e	+	a	3	e	+	a	4	e	+	a
[Δ		Δ	Δ		Δ	O	O	Δ		Δ		Δ	Δ	O	O]
R		L	R		L	R	L	R		L		R	L	R	L

As you learn a new part like this, you'll find yourself passing through predictable stages toward mastery. First, you won't be able to play the part *even with* conscious effort. Then you'll be able to play the part but *only with* conscious effort. Finally, you'll be able to play the part *without* conscious effort. Often you'll discover you've reached the third stage by accident when you look down and find your hands performing a complicated dance without you. At this point, the playing instructions have been transferred from your conscious mind to your body.

Once you can play a pattern unconsciously, you get to choose what you do with your conscious mind. You can focus on turning the notes into music. You can tune in to the spirit side of drumming. Or you can just relax and feel the rhythm. If you're playing in a group, you can also begin to listen to how all the parts fit together and open up to a sense of community with everyone around you.

Just be careful about listening to the lead drummer's solo. It's easy to get carried away and turned around. You may have noticed that already if you've tried playing along with the CD while Joh is soloing. So wait until you have your part down cold before you allow yourself the luxury of listening to the lead drummer.

Now here are the two parts from Djole combined on one chart:

PATTERNS 4-6 AND 5-3   **CD TRACK 4, R & L CHANNEL**

1	+	2	+	3	+	4	+	1	+	2	+	3	+	4	+	
[Δ		Δ	Δ		Δ	O	O	Δ		Δ		Δ	Δ	O	O]	Part 2
✳		Δ	Δ	✳]		[O	O	✳		Δ	Δ	✳]		[O	O	Part 1

Kassa part 1 and the swing feel

The pattern you're going to learn in this lesson is the first part from Kassa, a rhythm from Guinea traditionally played at harvest time to accompany workers in the fields. But this pattern doesn't appear only in Kassa – it's one of the most common djembe patterns in all of West African music. In fact, many of the patterns in this book appear in a wide variety of different rhythms. Whenever the same djembe patterns appear in different rhythms, it will be the **dundun** parts – parts played on double-headed, barrel-shaped bass drums – that give each rhythm its distinct character.

> **Whenever the same djembe patterns appear in different rhythms, it will be the dundun parts that give each rhythm its distinct character.**

To learn this part, start by listening to it on the CD. Notice that although there's a note on ONE – which is the first note you'll hear after the break – the repeating phrase actually starts on the AND of 2 and *ends* on 1:

PATTERN 6-1   CD TRACK 5, R CHANNEL

1	+	2	+	3	+	4	+	1	+	2	+	3	+	4	+
Δ]				[Δ	Δ		O	O	Δ]			[Δ	Δ		O	O
R				R	L		R	L	R			R	L		R	L

PATTERN 6-1 (IN 4/4)   CD TRACK 5, R CHANNEL

1	e	+	a	2	e	+	a	3	e	+	a	4	e	+	a
Δ]				[Δ	Δ		O	O	Δ]			[Δ	Δ		O	O
R				R	L		R	L	R			R	L		R	L

To remember the phrasing of this part, you can use the sentence "The DRUM leads the DANCE":

PATTERN 6-1   CD TRACK 5, R CHANNEL

1	+	2	+	3	+	4	+	1	+	2	+	3	+	4	+
Δ]				[Δ	Δ		O	O	Δ]			[Δ	Δ		O	O
DANCE.			The	DRUM		leads	the	DANCE.			The	DRUM		leads	the

Notice how the hand pattern used for this part reinforces the phrasing. You start with your right hand at the beginning of the phrase and alternate hands until the end – RLRLR. The break in the hand pattern – where you make two strokes in a row with your right hand – coincides with the break between phrases:

PATTERN 6-1   CD TRACK 5, R CHANNEL

1	+	2	+	3	+	4	+	1	+	2	+	3	+	4	+
Δ]				[Δ	Δ		O	O	Δ]			[Δ	Δ		O	O
R			R	L		R	L	R			R	L		R	L

When you listen to this part on the CD, you may notice that there's something going on with the timing of the strokes that isn't reflected on the chart. What you're hearing is Joh playing this part with what jazz musicians call a **swing feel**. To create a swing feel on a pattern in four, you play the notes on the ANDS slightly closer to the numbered beats. Here's how the part might look if we tried to indicate the swing feel on the chart:

PATTERN 6-1   CD TRACK 5, R CHANNEL

1	+	2	+	3	+	4	+	1	+	2	+	3	+	4	+
Δ]				[Δ	Δ		O	O	Δ]			[Δ	Δ		O	O
R			R	L		R	L	R			R	L		R	L

How far the notes on the ANDS are "swung" varies from rhythm to rhythm and from drummer to drummer. Joh played this part on the CD with a fairly pronounced swing because he was playing it relatively slowly. When the part is played fast, the swing becomes less pronounced and the timing evens out.

Musical time out: Offbeats and upbeats

The musical term for the ANDS on our charts in four is **offbeats**:

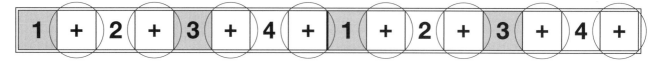

The numbered beats that fall exactly midway between pulses are called **upbeats**:

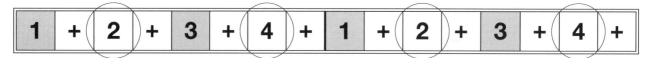

Once you're comfortable playing this part, you can use it to check in with your body. Play it at the fastest speed you can maintain for at least three minutes. Then focus on the muscles in your face. Is your jaw relaxed? How about your neck and shoulders? Now move down your arms. Are they relaxed? Are your wrists loose? Wherever you encounter tension on this route, consciously release it. To play fast, to play long, to play well – play relaxed.

To play fast, to play long, to play well – play relaxed.

Next check your breathing. *Are* you breathing? Good. When we first started drumming, whenever we had to play something difficult or fast, our lungs would shut down as if we were underwater. As soon as we came up for air, our playing improved. Make sure that your breathing always stays relaxed and regular, especially when you're under pressure.

Now check your posture. One way to do this is to watch yourself play in a mirror. Is your spine straight? Are your elbows close to your sides? Are your movements efficient and symmetrical? While you practice, keep asking yourself: What could be lighter, freer, easier?

PRACTICE PRINCIPLE

Practice in the mirror occasionally to check your posture and technique.

**Keep asking yourself:
What could be lighter, freer, easier?**

Kassa part 2 and ghost notes

The music of the djembe comes from the contrast between the three basic sounds. The bass, the tone, and the slap should sound as distinct from each other as possible.

The music of the djembe comes from the contrast between the three basic sounds.

The following exercise will give you a chance to practice making the three basic sounds. It will also give you another chance to practice moving your hands forward and backward on the drumhead. Go slowly at first. Focus on technique while you play. When you're able to make your bass, tone, and slap really sound different from one another, the exercise becomes a beautiful song:

PATTERN 7-1

1	+	2	+	3	+	4	+	1	+	2	+	3	+	4	+
O	O	▲	▲	✳	✳	▲	▲	O	O	▲	▲	✳	✳	▲	▲
R	L	R	L	R	L	R	L	R	L	R	L	R	L	R	L

In a minute we'll turn this exercise into the second part from Kassa. But first you need to know about ghost notes. **Ghost notes** are barely audible or inaudible touches that help you keep steady time. They structure the silence between the main strokes of a pattern. When you fill in every empty beat with ghost notes, your hands become your metronome.

When you fill in every empty beat with ghost notes, your hands become your metronome.

Ghost notes are relaxed strokes. All you do is touch the drumhead lightly with the pads of your fingertips. You can do this with your

palms held off the drumhead or resting on the edge of the drum.
Try them both ways as you play the following exercise:

PATTERN 7-2

1	+	2	+	3	+	4	+	1	+	2	+	3	+	4	+
•	•	•	•	•	•	•	•	•	•	•	•	•	•	•	•
R	L	R	L	R	L	R	L	R	L	R	L	R	L	R	L

Ghost notes can be used like training wheels, which is how you're going to use them in this lesson. You'll put them on while you're learning the second part from Kassa and take them off once you feel secure with the timing of the main strokes.

• = ghost note or touch

Here's the second part from Kassa with a ghost note on 3 in each measure. This pattern is the same as the first exercise in this lesson except that the ghost notes on 3 have replaced the bass strokes. Remember to keep a pulse going somewhere in your body as you play this pattern. You're going to need it:

PATTERN 7-3

1	+	2	+	3	+	4	+	1	+	2	+	3	+	4	+
O	O	Δ	Δ	•	✳	Δ	Δ	O	O	Δ	Δ	•	✳	Δ	Δ
R	L	R	L	R	L	R	L	R	L	R	L	R	L	R	L

Did you find it hard to keep track of the pulse? Did it drift from the first of the two tones to the slap on 4? If so, that's because what used to be a continuous pattern starting *on* the pulse, is now two identical shorter phrases starting and ending *off* the pulse. And each of those phrases starts in one measure and ends in the next, with the pulse on 1 buried in the middle:

PATTERN 7-3

1	+	2	+	3	+	4	+	1	+	2	+	3	+	4	+
O	O	Δ	Δ]	•	[✻	Δ	Δ	O	O	Δ	Δ]	•	[✻	Δ	Δ
R	L	R	L	R	L	R	L	R	L	R	L	R	L	R	L

Whenever a repeating phrase starts and ends off the pulse, it can be disorienting, especially when you play a pattern in isolation, as you just did. When you play this part along with the first part from Kassa on the CD, you'll have reference points in that part that will help you keep your bearings. In a full ensemble, you'd also get reference points from the bell and dundun parts.

But by itself this pattern is inherently ambiguous. It gives you no clues about where the pulse is. This kind of rhythmic ambiguity is typical of African music. Although the rhythms are organized around a pulse, the pulse is often implied rather than played, felt rather than heard. That's why we've been recommending that you keep a pulse going somewhere in your body while you play.

In African music, the pulse is often implied rather than played, felt rather than heard.

To help you keep track of the pulse in this pattern while you're learning it, say the sentence "Here is the PULSE and two slaps" while you play. Start on ONE with the fragment "PULSE and two slaps" and continue from there with the full phrase:

PATTERN 7-3

1	+	2	+	3	+	4	+	1	+	2	+	3	+	4	+
O	O	Δ	Δ]	•	[✻	Δ	Δ	O	O	Δ	Δ]	•	[✻	Δ	Δ
PULSE	and	two	slaps.		Here	is	the	PULSE	and	two	slaps.		Here	is	the

Now you're ready to play the second part from Kassa without ghost notes. You'll notice on the CD that this part has a swing just like the swing in the first part from Kassa. To get that swing in your playing, all you have to do is play the notes on the ANDs slightly closer to the numbered beats. After the break you start playing on ONE:

PATTERN 7-4 CD TRACK 5, L CHANNEL

1	+	2	+	3	+	4	+	1	+	2	+	3	+	4	+
O	O	△	△]		[✳	△	△	O	O	△	△]		[✳	△	△
R	L	R	L		L	R	L	R	L	R	L		L	R	L

PATTERN 7-4 (IN 4/4) CD TRACK 5, L CHANNEL

1	e	+	a	2	e	+	a	3	e	+	a	4	e	+	a
O	O	△	△]		[✳	△	△	O	O	△	△]		[✳	△	△
R	L	R	L		L	R	L	R	L	R	L		L	R	L

While this part on the CD may seem fast to you at first, Joh actually played it slower than its customary tempo. If after practicing this part on your own without the CD you still can't keep up with the tempo, you can simplify the part by taking out the bass strokes:

PATTERN 7-5

1	+	2	+	3	+	4	+	1	+	2	+	3	+	4	+
O	O	△	△]			[△	△	O	O	△	△]			[△	△
R	L	R	L			R	L	R	L	R	L			R	L

Knowing how to simplify a pattern that's moving too fast is an essential survival skill for beginners. When you play with a group – where you may be expected to play a part at blazing speed for an hour or more without stopping – it's always better to simplify a pattern by omitting notes than to play any note out of time. And – because they're quieter than tones and slaps – the first candidates for omission when you simplify are bass tones. Just remember that simplifying is a last resort – it's no substitute for practicing the real part.

It's better to simplify a pattern by omitting notes than to play any note out of time.

Now here are the two parts from Kassa combined on one chart. Notice how they overlap. The second part ends where the first begins – on the AND of 2:

PATTERNS 6-1 & 7-4   CD TRACK 5, R & L CHANNEL

1	+	2	+	3	+	4	+	1	+	2	+	3	+	4	+
O	O	Δ	Δ]		[✳	Δ	Δ	O	O	Δ	Δ]		[✳	Δ	Δ
Δ]			[Δ	Δ		O	O	Δ]			[Δ	Δ		O	O

Part 2 (second row), Part 1 (third row)

If you haven't done it yet, try playing this rhythm over and over for as long as you can. The rhythm you play for a minute becomes a different rhythm when you play it for an hour. Repetition triggers mysterious processes in the body and mind. That's why repetitive rhythms play a critical role in the sacred rituals of so many cultures, often inducing a state of trance in the participants. We don't talk much about the trance effect of repetition. We just give you the rhythms and let you experience it for yourself.

The rhythm you play for a minute becomes a different rhythm when you play it for an hour.

Madan parts 1 & 2 and adding bass strokes

In this lesson you'll be learning two parts from Madan, a rhythm from Mali played at social gatherings and celebrations. You should find it easy, because the new parts are created by simply adding bass strokes to two patterns you already know. And you should have plenty of time to get in those extra strokes, because Madan is usually played at a medium tempo.

The first part you'll modify is the first part from Kassa. To refresh your memory, here's how that pattern looks:

PATTERN 6-1　　　　　　　　　　**CD TRACK 5, R CHANNEL**

1	+	2	+	3	+	4	+	1	+	2	+	3	+	4	+
Δ]				[Δ	Δ		O	O	Δ]			[Δ	Δ		O	O
R				R	L		R	L	R			R	L		R	L

When you add a bass stroke on 2 in each measure, you get the first part from Madan. Notice that the hand pattern stays the same. You just start the phrase one beat earlier with your left hand:

PATTERN 8-1　　　　　　　　　　**CD TRACK 6, R CHANNEL**

1	+	2	+	3	+	4	+	1	+	2	+	3	+	4	+
Δ]		[✳	Δ	Δ		O	O	Δ]		[✳	Δ	Δ		O	O
R		L	R	L		R	L	R		L	R	L		R	L

PATTERN 8-1 (IN 4/4)　　　　　　**CD TRACK 6, R CHANNEL**

1	e	+	a	2	e	+	a	3	e	+	a	4	e	+	a
Δ]		[✳	Δ	Δ		O	O	Δ]		[✳	Δ	Δ		O	O
R		L	R	L		R	L	R		L	R	L		R	L

The second part you'll modify is the second part from Kuku. Here's how that pattern looks:

PATTERN 2-5   CD TRACK 2, L CHANNEL

1	+	2	+	3	+	4	+	1	+	2	+	3	+	4	+
*]		[O	O			Δ		*]		[O	O			Δ	
L		R	L			R		L		R	L			R	

When you add a bass stroke on the AND of 3 in each measure, you get the second part from Madan. Again the hand pattern of the original part stays the same. You just insert an extra stroke in the left hand in the middle of the phrase:

PATTERN 8-2   CD TRACK 6, L CHANNEL

1	+	2	+	3	+	4	+	1	+	2	+	3	+	4	+
*]		[O	O		*	Δ		*]		[O	O		*	Δ	
L		R	L		L	R		L		R	L		L	R	

PATTERN 8-2 (IN 4/4)   CD TRACK 6, L CHANNEL

1	e	+	a	2	e	+	a	3	e	+	a	4	e	+	a
*]			[O	O		*	Δ	*]			[O	O		*	Δ
L			R	L		L	R	L			R	L		L	R

Here are both parts on a single chart. Notice that both phrases begin on 2 and end on 1. When you listen to these parts on the CD, you'll hear Joh play them both with a slight swing feel:

PATTERN 8-1 & 8-2   CD TRACK 6, R & L CHANNEL

1	+	2	+	3	+	4	+	1	+	2	+	3	+	4	+	
✻]		[O	O		✻	Δ		✻]		[O	O		✻	<u>Δ</u>		Part 2
Δ]		[✻	Δ	Δ		O	O	Δ]		[✻	Δ	Δ		O	O	Part 1

Since this is a short lesson, it might be a good time to go back and review the patterns you've learned so far. We know it's tempting to learn as many new rhythms as possible as fast as possible. They're like narcotics; the more you get, the more you want. Before you know it, you're a rhythm junkie, trying to score wherever you can. We admit we were once powerless over our urge to learn to play everything we heard. With help from our teachers, we are now on the path to recovery, one rhythm at a time. Don't play a mile wide and an inch deep. Learn a few rhythms well.

**Don't play a mile wide and an inch deep.
Learn a few rhythms well.**

The breaks in four and the flam

In traditional West African settings, drumming usually begins with a period of unstructured improvisation before each djembe player settles into a specific part. In non-traditional settings such as concerts, drum and dance performances, and classes, breaks are played by a lead djembe player to signal all the drummers to begin playing their parts at the same time. Breaks may also be used to signal a change in tempo or rhythm, to punctuate the entrance or exit of a dancer, and to bring a rhythm to a close.

Before you can play the break in four you've been hearing on the CD, you need to know how to make a **flam**. A flam is a double stroke in which both hands play almost simultaneously with equal intensity. One hand plays *just before* the beat and the other *directly on* the beat.

To learn the break in four, you need to learn how to make a flam with two open tones. To hear how this should sound, put on the CD and play any rhythm in four. The first thing you'll hear is a flam with two open tones.

Now practice playing flams on each pulse. Start by playing the note just before the beat with your left hand and the note on the beat with your right. Make sure both hands land almost simultaneously with equal intensity:

PATTERN 9-1

1	+	2	+	3	+	4	+	1	+	2	+	3	+	4	+
⁰Ȯ				⁰Ȯ				⁰Ȯ				⁰Ȯ			
LR				LR				LR				LR			

Next try reversing your hands, so that your right hand plays the note just before the beat and your left hand plays the note on the beat:

PATTERN 9-2

1	+	2	+	3	+	4	+	1	+	2	+	3	+	4	+
°O				°O				°O				°O			
RL				RL				RL				RL			

Now here's the full break. Notice that you start with your left hand and continue alternating hands all the way through. Go slow at first and count out loud while you play to make sure you get the timing right:

PATTERN 9-3

1	+	2	+	3	+	4	+	1	+	2	+	3	+	4	+
°O		O	O	O				O	O	Δ	Δ	Δ			
LR		L	R	L				R	L	R	L	R			

If you found it easier to play the flam starting with your right hand, just reverse the hands all the way through:

PATTERN 9-4

1	+	2	+	3	+	4	+	1	+	2	+	3	+	4	+
°O		O	O	O				O	O	Δ	Δ	Δ			
RL		R	L	R				L	R	L	R	L			

Notice that both of these patterns use **alternating hands**. It's the hand-pattern strategy you've been using on most of the patterns in this book. It's an easy strategy: regardless of which hand starts, right is followed by left and left by right. It's as simple as walking.

There are other hand-pattern strategies. For example, some drummers believe you should play any note that falls on the pulse with your strong hand. Other drummers strategize so they can play a particular slap in a pattern with their strong hand.

Don't get hung up trying to figure out the "correct" hand pattern to use on a rhythm. Different strategies have different objectives. Ultimately, the best hand-pattern strategy is the one that helps you produce the best sound the most consistently with the least amount of stress and strain.

Ultimately, the best hand-pattern strategy is the one that helps you produce the best sound the most consistently with the least amount of stress and strain.

Now let's go back to the break. If you want to start *and* end on your right hand, you need to break the flow of alternating hands somewhere in the middle of the pattern. Here are a couple of ways to do it:

PATTERN 9-5

1	+	2	+	3	+	4	+	1	+	2	+	3	+	4	+
°O		O	O		O			O	O	△	△	△			
RL		R	L		R			R	L	R	L	R			

PATTERN 9-6

1	+	2	+	3	+	4	+	1	+	2	+	3	+	4	+
°O		O	O		O			O	O	△	△	△			
RL		R	L		R			L	R	R	L	R			

Another popular break in four replaces the three slaps with two tones on 2 and 3 in the second measure. Because this break has one less stroke, you can start and end with your right hand without having to break the flow of alternating hands in the middle:

1	+	2	+	3	+	4	+	1	+	2	+	3	+	4	+
Ô		O	O		O			O	O		O		O		
RL		R	L		R			L	R		L		R		

May the time not be distant when the people you play with trust you enough to ask you to play the break that brings everyone in.

CHAPTER 6

West African rhythms in six

lesson **10**

Suku part 1 & 2 and the pulse in six

For those of us raised in the rock and pop world of four, the African world of six is uncharted territory. By **six** we mean two measures of **6/8 time**, where there are 6 eighth notes to a measure and each eighth note gets one beat. The pulse falls on beats 1 and 4 in each measure. And each pulse is divided into three beats:

1	2	3	4	5	6	1	2	3	4	5	6

Musical time out: Counting in six

We could have counted patterns in six in a single measure of 12 eighth notes. This way of counting is called **12/8 time** and it looks like this:

1	+	a	2	+	a	3	+	a	4	+	a

Counting in 12/8 has the advantage of putting the pulse on each numbered beat. But we chose to chart in 6/8 for several reasons. We find it's easier to work with two short 6-beat measures than with one long 12-beat measure. We also like the counting system in 6/8 better because each beat gets its own number. Rhythms in 6/8 are also a lot easier to talk about than rhythms in 12/8. (You already know how we feel about referring to the "uh" of 4.)

If you're used to counting in 12/8 and don't want to change, that's fine. Just think of each two-measure chart as a single measure of 12/8 instead. This won't change the sound or the speed of the patterns. And to help you out, in each lesson we've included a chart in 12/8 for whatever part is the subject of the lesson.

Start by playing the pulse in six with bass tones while you count out loud "**1**, 2, 3, **4**, 5, 6." Keep a pulse going somewhere in your body and feel how each pulse is divided into three beats:

PATTERN 10-1

1	2	3	4	5	6	1	2	3	4	5	6
✳			✳			✳			✳		
R			L			R			L		

Now replace the bass strokes with slaps and fill in the empty beats with ghost notes. Notice that when you make a stroke on every beat in six with alternating hands, the pulse moves back and forth between your right hand and your left. Remember to try to make the slaps sound the same in both hands:

PATTERN 10-2

1	2	3	4	5	6	1	2	3	4	5	6
Δ	•	•	Δ	•	•	Δ	•	•	Δ	•	•
R	L	R	L	R	L	R	L	R	L	R	L

Now replace the ghost notes on 5 and 6 with open tones:

PATTERN 10-3

1	2	3	4	5	6	1	2	3	4	5	6
△	•	•	△	O	O	△	•	•	△	O	O
R	L	R	L	R	L	R	L	R	L	R	L

When you take out the ghost notes, you'll be playing the first part from Suku, another rhythm from Mali played at social gatherings and celebrations. Notice that each phrase starts on 4 and ends on 1:

PATTERN 10-4   **CD TRACK 7, R CHANNEL**

1	2	3	4	5	6	1	2	3	4	5	6
△]			[△	O	O	△]			[△	O	O
R			L	R	L	R			L	R	L

When you listen to this part on the CD, first you'll hear the break in six which ends on 4 in the second measure. Then the part starts with the slap on ONE – which is just a fragment of the phrase – before the full phrase starts on 4.

Here's how the first part from Suku looks charted in 12/8 time:

PATTERN 10-4 (IN 12/8)   **CD TRACK 7, R CHANNEL**

1	+	a	2	+	a	3	+	a	4	+	a
△]			[△	O	O	△]			[△	O	O
R			L	R	L	R			L	R	L

To get ready to play the second part from Suku, start by playing slaps on the pulse with just your right hand:

1	2	3	4	5	6	1	2	3	4	5	6
△			△			△			△		
R			R			R			R		

Now add a bass stroke in the left hand on 6 in each measure:

PATTERN 10-6

1	2	3	4	5	6	1	2	3	4	5	6
△			△		✳	△			△		✳
R			R		L	R			R		L

When you add an open tone in the left hand on 3 in each measure you'll be playing the second part from Suku. This means that your left hand plays on the beat before each pulse, moving back and forth between the bass stroke and the open tone. To make sure you continue to feel the pulse in your right hand, keep a pulse going somewhere in your body. You can also count out loud while you play. You start playing on ONE, but the phrase starts on 6 and ends on 4:

PATTERN 10-7 CD TRACK 7, L CHANNEL

1	2	3	4	5	6	1	2	3	4	5	6
△		O	△]		[✳	△		O	△]		[✳
R		L	R		L	R		L	R		L

PATTERN 10-7 (IN 12/8) CD TRACK 7, L CHANNEL

1	+	a	2	+	a	3	+	a	4	+	a
△		O	△]		[✳	△		O	△]		[✳
R		L	R		L	R		L	R		L

Playing this part for an extended period of time can be tough on your right hand. If it starts to get sore, you can simplify the part by taking out the bass stroke and changing the hand pattern so you play the slaps in alternating hands. Just remember that when you do this, you're not technically playing Suku anymore (although you are playing a part that appears in many other West African rhythms in six):

PATTERN 10-8

1	2	3	4	5	6	1	2	3	4	5	6
[Δ		O	Δ]			[Δ		O	Δ]		
R		R	L			R		R	L		

PLAYING PRINCIPLE

Don't play in pain.

Whatever you do, don't play in pain. If your hands – or your wrists or your elbows – start to hurt, stop playing. Before you start playing again, analyze and eliminate the problem. If you can't figure it out yourself, find a good teacher and take some private lessons. If you continue to play on an injured hand, you may do serious damage. You've got a long drumming career ahead of you. Don't jeopardize it by playing in pain.

Here are both parts from Suku on a single chart. Notice that although the slaps in both parts fall on the pulse, the phrasing of each part is different. The first part *starts* on 4 while the second part *ends* there:

PATTERNS 10-4 AND 10-7   **CD TRACK 7, R & L CHANNEL**

	1	2	3	4	5	6	1	2	3	4	5	6
Part 2	Δ		O	Δ]		[✳	Δ		O	Δ]		[✳
Part 1	Δ]			[Δ	O	O	Δ]			[Δ	O	O

As you listen to these two parts together on the CD, you'll hear the melody created by the open tones moving between the two parts.

lesson **11**

Sunguru Bani parts 1, 2, & 3
and the polyrhythm 3 over 2

In this lesson, you'll learn Joh Camara's arrangement of Sunguru Bani (soon-goo-roo bah-nee), another rhythm from Mali played at social gatherings and celebrations. There are three parts to this rhythm. The following exercise will get you ready for the first part. You'll play bass strokes on the pulse and open tones on the offbeats – the beats between pulses:

PATTERN 11-1

1	2	3	4	5	6	1	2	3	4	5	6
✳	O	O	✳	O	O	✳	O	O	✳	O	O
R	L	R	L	R	L	R	L	R	L	R	L

To create the first part from Sunguru Bani, take out the second pair of tones in each measure and put a slap on 5. You start playing on ONE, which is also the start of the phrase:

PATTERN 11-2   **CD TRACK 8, R CHANNEL**

1	2	3	4	5	6	1	2	3	4	5	6
[✳	O	O	✳	▲]		[✳	O	O	✳	▲]	
R	L	R	L	R		R	L	R	L	R	

PATTERN 11-2 (IN 12/8)   **CD TRACK 8, R CHANNEL**

1	+	a	2	+	a	3	+	a	4	+	a
[✳	O	O	✳	▲]		[✳	O	O	✳	▲]	
R	L	R	L	R		R	L	R	L	R	

The second part from Sunguru Bani has bass strokes on the pulse just like the first part. You also start playing this part on ONE, but notice that the phrase starts on 3 and ends on 1. Also notice how the hand pattern reinforces the phrasing. You start with your right hand at the beginning of the phrase and alternate hands until the end – RLRLR. The break in the hand pattern – where you make two strokes in a row with your right hand – coincides with the break between phrases:

PATTERN 11-3   CD TRACK 8, L CHANNEL

1	2	3	4	5	6	1	2	3	4	5	6
✳]		[Δ	✳	O	O	✳]		[Δ	✳	O	O
R		R	L	R	L	R		R	L	R	L

PATTERN 11-3 (IN 12/8)   CD TRACK 8, L CHANNEL

1	+	a	2	+	a	3	+	a	4	+	a
✳]		[Δ	✳	O	O	✳]		[Δ	✳	O	O
R		R	L	R	L	R		R	L	R	L

In the third part from Sunguru Bani, the pulse stays in your right hand instead of alternating between right and left. To get ready for this part, start by playing the pulse with your right hand, alternating between slaps and tones:

PATTERN 11-4

1	2	3	4	5	6	1	2	3	4	5	6
Δ			O			Δ			O		
R			R			R			R		

Now add a bass stroke in the left hand on 3 in each measure:

PATTERN 11-5

1	2	3	4	5	6	1	2	3	4	5	6
Δ		✳	O			Δ		✳	O		
R		L	R			R		L	R		

When you add a tone in your left hand on 5 in each measure, you'll be playing the third part from Sunguru Bani. You start playing on ONE, but the phrase starts on 3 and ends on 1, like the phrase in the second part:

PATTERN 11-6   CD TRACK 9, R CHANNEL

1	2	3	4	5	6	1	2	3	4	5	6
Δ]		[✳	O	O		Δ]		[✳	O	O	
R		L	R	L		R		L	R	L	

PATTERN 11-6 (IN 12/8)   CD TRACK 9, R CHANNEL

1	+	a	2	+	a	3	+	a	4	+	a
Δ]		[✳	O	O		Δ]		[✳	O	O	
R		L	R	L		R		L	R	L	

Because the phrase starts with the bass stroke in your left hand, it's easy to get turned around and start feeling the bass stroke as the pulse – especially if you play this part in isolation. To make sure you keep feeling the pulse in your right hand, say the sentence "The PULSE is HERE" while you play:

PATTERN 11-6   **CD TRACK 9, R CHANNEL**

1	2	3	4	5	6	1	2	3	4	5	6
Δ]		[✳	O	O		Δ]		[✳	O	O	
HERE.		The	PULSE	is		HERE.		The	PULSE	is	

Here are all three parts on a single chart:

PATTERNS 11-2, 11-3, & 11-6   **CD TRACK 9, R & L CHANNEL**

	1	2	3	4	5	6	1	2	3	4	5	6
Part 3	Δ]		[✳	O	O		Δ]		[✳	O	O	
Part 2	✳]		[Δ	✳	O	O	✳]		[Δ	✳	O	O
Part 1	[✳	O	O	✳	Δ]		[✳	O	O	✳	Δ]	

Embedded within Sunguru Bani is the polyrhythm 3 over 2. In simple terms, a **polyrhythm** is created when two different pulses are played at the same time. If this simplified definition still sounds confusing, don't worry. We'll walk you through it step by step.

To start, remember that a pulse is metronomic, which means that the individual pulses are evenly-spaced. We call the pulse in six you've been working with so far the **4-pulse** because there are four evenly-spaced pulses in a two-measure cycle. This is the underlying pulse in Sunguru Bani. This 4-pulse is played with bass strokes on beats 1 and 4 in each measure in both the first and second parts:

1	2	3	4	5	6	1	2	3	4	5	6
Δ]		[*	O	O		Δ]		[*	O	O	
*]		[Δ	*	O	O	*]		[Δ	*	O	O
[*	O	O	*	Δ]		[*	O	O	*	Δ]	

To make it easier for you to see this 4-pulse, in the next chart we've taken out all the other strokes from the first and second parts and just left the bass strokes on a single row:

PATTERN 11-7

1	2	3	4	5	6	1	2	3	4	5	6
*			*			*			*		

The second pulse in Sunguru Bani is created by the six evenly-spaced slaps in the rhythm. These slaps are distributed throughout all three parts, and they fall on beats 1, 3, and 5 in each measure:

1	2	3	4	5	6	1	2	3	4	5	6
Δ]		[*	O	O		Δ]		[*	O	O	
*]		[Δ	*	O	O	*]		[Δ	*	O	O
[*	O	O	*	Δ]		[*	O	O	*	Δ]	

We've combined these slaps on a single row in the following chart:

PATTERN 11-8

1	2	3	4	5	6	1	2	3	4	5	6
Δ		Δ		Δ		Δ		Δ		Δ	

Since there are six evenly-spaced slaps in the two-measure cycle, we call the pulse created by these slaps a **6-pulse**.

When you put the 6 slaps over the 4 bass strokes, you get the polyrhythm 6 over 4 or – taken one measure at a time – 3 over 2. This is the polyrhythm at the heart of Sunguru Bani:

PATTERN 11-9

1	2	3	4	5	6	1	2	3	4	5	6
△		△		△		△		△		△	
✳			✳			✳			✳		

The easiest way to feel the polyrhythm 3 over 2 is to play the 3 with one hand and the 2 with the other. You don't even need a drum. Just find a different surface for each hand so you can make two different sounds.

You can even practice directly on your body. To get two different sounds, play one part on your thigh and the other on your chest. If you play the 3 with your right hand and the 2 with your left, the hand pattern becomes "together-right-left-right; together-right-left-right":

PATTERN 11-10

1	2	3	4	5	6	1	2	3	4	5	6
X		X		X		X		X		X	
X			X			X			X		

You can practice polyrhythms anywhere: in a check-out line, in a waiting room, in rush-hour traffic. Why kill time when you can play with it instead?

Why kill time when you can play with it instead?

lesson

Tiriba, parts 1, 2, & 3 and the 6/8 bell

In this lesson you'll learn three parts from Tiriba, a rhythm from Guinea traditionally played at circumcisions and other important ceremonies and celebrations. The first part is the easiest. Notice that your right hand is on the pulse:

PATTERN 12-1　　　　　　　　　　**CD TRACK 10, R CHANNEL**

1	2	3	4	5	6	1	2	3	4	5	6
[Δ		O	O]			[Δ		O	O]		
R		L	R			R		L	R		

PATTERN 12-1 (IN 12/8)　　　　　　**CD TRACK 10, R CHANNEL**

1	+	a	2	+	a	3	+	a	4	+	a
[Δ		O	O]			[Δ		O	O]		
R		L	R			R		L	R		

The second part from Tiriba is the most complicated pattern in this book. To make it easier to learn we've broken it in half. You already know the first measure. It's the same as the second part from Sunguru Bani. Here it is repeated twice:

PATTERN 11-3　　　　　　　　　　**CD TRACK 8, L CHANNEL**

1	2	3	4	5	6	1	2	3	4	5	6
*]		[Δ	*	O	O	*]		[Δ	*	O	O
R		R	L	R	L	R		R	L	R	L

Here's the second measure of the second part from Tiriba repeated twice. Start slow and count out loud at first to make sure you get the timing right:

PATTERN 12-2

1	2	3	4	5	6	1	2	3	4	5	6
✳	△		O		O	✳	△		O		O
R	L		R		L	R	L		R		L

Once you're comfortable with both halves of the part, you're ready to put them together. When you combine them, watch out for the placement of the two slaps. The first slap falls on 3 in the right hand and the second falls on 2 in the left. Also notice the phrasing. After the break you start playing on ONE, but the phrase starts on 3 and ends on ONE:

PATTERN 12-3   **CD TRACK 10, L CHANNEL**

1	2	3	4	5	6	1	2	3	4	5	6
✳]		[△	✳	O	O	✳	△		O		O
R		R	L	R	L	R	L		R		L

PATTERN 12-3 (IN 12/8)   **CD TRACK 10, L CHANNEL**

1	+	a	2	+	a	3	+	a	4	+	a
✳]		[△	✳	O	O	✳	△		O		O
R		R	L	R	L	R	L		R		L

Notice how the hand pattern reinforces the phrasing. You start on 3 in the first measure with your right hand and alternate hands all the way through. The only break in the pattern of alternating hands – where you play two rights in a row – occurs *in between* where the phrase ends and where it begins again.

This second part from Tiriba tracks the pattern commonly called the 6/8 bell (also known as "the short bell"). This bell pattern is played with many African rhythms in six and is widely used in Afro-Cuban rhythms.

We've indicated the 6/8 bell with X's on the following chart above the second part from Tiriba so you can see how closely they match up. The only notes in the part from Tiriba that aren't in the 6/8 bell are the bass strokes on 4 in the first measure and 1 in the second:

PATTERN 12-4

1	2	3	4	5	6	1	2	3	4	5	6
X		X		X	X		X		X		X
✳		▲	✳	O	O	✳	▲		O		O

If you're looking for a fun challenge to work on when you can't play your drum, try putting the 6/8 bell in one hand and the 4-pulse in the other:

PATTERN 12-5

1	2	3	4	5	6	1	2	3	4	5	6
X		X		X	X		X		X		X
X			X			X			X		

Now for the third part from Tiriba. Since it's another two-measure pattern, we've broken it in half. On the next chart, we've repeated the first measure twice. Make sure you feel the pulse while you play it. The pulse on 1 is no problem because you play a bass stroke there. But feeling the pulse on 4 is tricky because you don't play anything on that beat. It helps if you can find a way to feel that silent pulse as part of the pattern:

PATTERN 12-6

1	2	3	4	5	6	1	2	3	4	5	6
✳	◭	O		◭		✳	◭	O		◭	
L	R	L		R		L	R	L		R	

In the next chart, we've repeated the second measure of the pattern twice. It's just bass strokes in the left hand on the pulse followed by slaps in the right hand on the beat after each pulse. Make sure you keep feeling the pulse in your *left* hand rather than your right:

PATTERN 12-7

1	2	3	4	5	6	1	2	3	4	5	6
✳	◭		✳	◭		✳	◭		✳	◭	
L	R		L	R		L	R		L	R	

Now you're ready to combine the two halves and play the third part from Tiriba. Notice that the right hand continues to play steadily on the beat after each pulse. Also notice that both the part and the phrase start on ONE:

PATTERN 12-8   **CD TRACK 11, R CHANNEL**

1	2	3	4	5	6	1	2	3	4	5	6
[✳	◭	O		◭		✳	◭		✳	◭]	
L	R	L		R		L	R		L	R	

1	+	a	2	+	a	3	+	a	4	+	a
[✳	Δ	O		Δ		✳	Δ		✳	Δ]	
L	R	L		R		L	R		L	R	

Here are all three parts from Tiriba combined on a single chart:

PATTERNS 12-1, 12-3, 12-8   CD TRACK 11, R & L CHANNEL

1	2	3	4	5	6	1	2	3	4	5	6	
[✳	Δ	O		Δ		✳	Δ		✳	Δ]		Part 3
✳]		[Δ	✳	O	O	✳	Δ		O		O	Part 2
[Δ		O	O]			[Δ		O	O]			Part 1

We've always agreed that if our house were on fire and we could only take one rhythm with us, the 6/8 bell would definitely be it. Then a couple years ago, Ken Dalluge, a percussionist from Santa Cruz, amazed us by pointing out the correspondence between the structure of this universal rhythmic pattern and the structure of the major scale.

This correspondence is easiest to understand if you think of the boxes on one of our charts in six as the keys on a piano, with the box on ONE as middle C. The notes of the bell pattern line up perfectly with the white keys on the piano. Where there's an empty box on the chart, there's a black key on the piano.

This correspondence is either one of the most amazing coincidences in the history of the planet or it reflects a mysterious underlying unity between rhythm and tonality.

HOW TO PLAY DJEMBE: WEST AFRICAN RHYTHMS FOR BEGINNERS

The breaks in six and sixteenth notes

On the CD, there are two different breaks in six: one for Suku and another for Sunguru Bani and Tiriba. The break that introduces Suku is the simpler of the two, so we'll start there.

The basic structure of the pattern is the pulse and the beat before each pulse. Before you play the break itself, start by playing each pulse with your right hand and the beat before each pulse with your left. All the notes are open tones:

PATTERN 13-1

1	2	3	4	5	6	1	2	3	4	5	6
O			O	O		O	O		O	O		O
R			L	R		L	R		L	R		L

Now play the same pattern with your hands reversed. Play each pulse with your left hand and the beat before each pulse with your right:

PATTERN 13-2

1	2	3	4	5	6	1	2	3	4	5	6
O			O	O		O	O		O	O		O
L			R	L		R	L		R	L		R

Each hand pattern has its advantages. The first allows you to play each pulse with your strong hand. The second allows you to start each pair of notes with your strong hand. (We're assuming you're right-handed. If you're left-handed, the advantages are reversed.) Pick the one that feels best to you.

To turn this pattern into the first break in six, all you need to do is start with a flam – just as you did for the break in four – and then end the pattern on 4 in the second measure. Here's the break with the right hand on the pulse:

PATTERN 13-3

1	2	3	4	5	6	1	2	3	4	5	6
°O		O	O			O	O		O	O	
LR		L	R			L	R		L	R	

PATTERN 13-3 (IN 12/8)

1	+	a	2	+	a	3	+	a	4	+	a
°O		O	O			O	O		O	O	
LR		L	R			L	R		L	R	

Here's the same break with the left hand on the pulse:

PATTERN 13-3

1	2	3	4	5	6	1	2	3	4	5	6
°O		O	O			O	O		O	O	
RL		R	L			R	L		R	L	

The second break in six introduces Sunguru Bani and Tiriba on the CD. It's created by taking two notes out of the 6/8 bell pattern. We've put the full 6/8 bell on the next chart with open tones and crossed out those two notes:

PATTERN 13-4

1	2	3	4	5	6	1	2	3	4	5	6
O		O		⊘	O		O		O		⊘

Now here's the break with the hand pattern underneath. Because it has five notes, you can start and end with your right hand. To get the feel for this pattern, it may help to hear the full 6/8 bell in your head while you play. Count out loud if you need to:

PATTERN 13-5

1	2	3	4	5	6	1	2	3	4	5	6
O		O			O		O		O		
R		L			R		L		R		

PATTERN 13-5 (IN 12/8)

1	+	a	2	+	a	3	+	a	4	+	a
O		O			O		O		O		
R		L			R		L		R		

Now we're going to teach a third break in six that isn't on the CD. It starts with a pair of **sixteenth notes**. Two sixteenth notes are equal to one eighth note, so you need to play them twice as fast. (If you've been counting in sixteenth notes all along, our sixteenth notes will be thirty-second notes to you.) We chart sixteenth notes as two notes within a single eighth-note box.

The next pattern is an exercise to get you ready for the third break. Each phrase starts with a pair of sixteenth notes on 1:

PATTERN 13-6

1	2	3	4	5	6	1	2	3	4	5	6
oo	O	O	O	O		oo	O	O	O	O	
RL	R	L	R	L		RL	R	L	R	L	

The third break – which is often used with Tiriba – is on the next chart. Notice that the first measure is the same as the pattern you just played:

PATTERN 13-7

1	2	3	4	5	6	1	2	3	4	5	6
oo	O	O	O	O		O	O		O		
RL	R	L	R	L		R	L		R		

PATTERN 13-7 (IN 12/8)

1	+	a	2	+	a	3	+	a	4	+	a
oo	O	O	O	O		O	O		O		
RL	R	L	R	L		R	L		R		

Now you know several popular breaks that are used to introduce West African rhythms. But as we said earlier, breaks are also used to signal the end of a rhythm. To turn any of the breaks you've learned – in six or in four – into a break to end a rhythm, just add a two-slap flam on 1 in the following measure.

We've extended the break on the next chart to include a closing flam. The flam starts with the right hand, but you can start it with either hand:

PATTERN 13-8

1	2	3	4	5	6	1	2	3	4	5	6	1
oo	O	O	O	O		O	O		O			▵▵
RL	R	L	R	L		R	L		R			RL

CHAPTER 7

Tuning your djembe

When you're a beginner, it's hard to tell if your djembe is in tune. You need good technique on the basic strokes to be able to judge tuning, and good technique takes time to develop. The sounds of a djembe are also extremely complex. It takes a while to learn to analyze those sounds and hear subtle differences. So your ability to tune a djembe will naturally improve as you gain experience and get familiar with your drum. In the meantime, you might want to have your teacher or another experienced player tune your djembe for you.

The goal of tuning is to get the drumhead to a level of tension where slaps, open tones, and bass strokes all sound good. If the head is too loose, it will be hard to get a crisp slap. If it's too tight, the open tone may get choked and the bass may lose its bottom. Beyond this, tuning is a matter of personal preference. It's your drum. You're the one who's going to be playing it. So the most important thing is that it sounds good to you.

How you tune your djembe depends on what kind of djembe you have. If you have a djembe with a head held on with bolts adjusted from above, just go around the head tightening or loosening each one the same small amount in turn. Pick a distinctive place to start – such as the bolt that lines up with the name on the drum – so you'll know when you've gone all the way around. Adjusting the bolts equally and gradually will ensure that there's even pressure on the head, so the drum doesn't get pulled out of shape. To test whether the head is tightened evenly, go around it making a tone near each bolt. All the tones should be the same pitch. You can also look at the head from the side to make sure it's level.

If you've got a djembe with metal lugs that are adjusted along the side, the tuning procedure is basically the same as it is for tuning a djembe with bolts that are adjusted from above. The only difference is that clockwise and counterclockwise are reversed when you're adjusting lugs that pull down on the head from below. Here's how to remember which way to turn your wrench. With the djembe between your legs, attach the wrench to the lug directly in front of you. To tighten the lug, move the handle to the right; to loosen the lug, move the handle to the left. Tight to the right and loose to the left.

If you've got a traditional djembe that's tuned with ropes, there are many different ways of tuning it. All are confusing at first and a little hard to explain. We've picked the method we like best and that's what we'll be explaining to you. Our explanation will make the most sense if you've got your drum right in front of you and you follow along with each step.

The process of tightening with ropes is called **pulling a diamond** because when one rope is pulled over another it creates a diamond shape. To get ready to pull a diamond, the first thing you need to do is find the loose end of the rope on your drum. If it's wrapped around the base of your drum then unwrap it. If it's threaded behind ropes, unthread it until it's coming through the center of the last pulled diamond.

Now check to see which direction you're going to be pulling. If you're heading to the left with your next diamond, refer to the first diagram below. If you're heading to the right, skip to the second diagram:

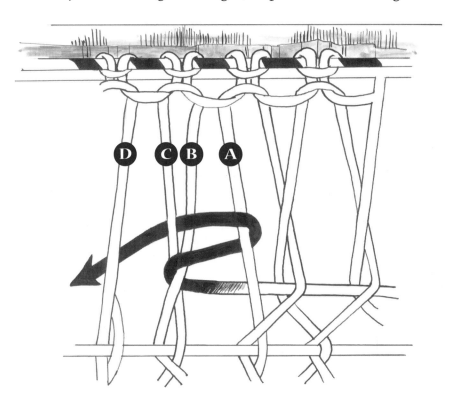

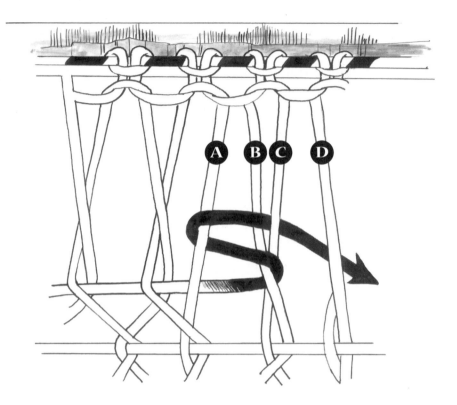

The rope pattern in these illustrations is called the **Mali weave**. Here's the formula for creating it: under 2, over 1, under 1, over 2. The illustrations above indicate an additional step of "under 2," which keeps your first diamond from coming loose after you've pulled it and becomes the first step towards creating the next diamond.

Now let's take it step at a time.

Under 2: Take the loose end of the rope and run it behind the next two vertical ropes, ropes A and B. If it's hard to get behind a vertical rope, use a screwdriver to hold it away from the drum.

Over 1: Bring the rope back over rope B, so you're heading in the opposite direction.

Under 1: Run the rope behind rope A.

Over 2: Bring the rope back over ropes A and B, heading in the original direction. Pull the rope down towards the bottom of the drum until it's horizontal.

Under 2: Run the rope behind the next two vertical ropes, ropes C and D. (Ropes C and D will become ropes A and B of the next diamond.)

Now you're ready to pull the diamond. Lay your drum down on a surface where it won't get scratched, with the base of the drum towards you. Then wrap the rope around a sturdy stick or a hammer so it won't dig into your hands when you pull. Now sit down and brace the drum with your feet. Then lean back and pull the rope out and down towards the base of the drum. A diamond will magically appear. And because you've run the rope behind the next two vertical ropes, your diamond won't come out.

Some drummers believe it's important to pull a whole row at one time so there's even pressure on the head. If you want to get even pressure on the head without pulling so many diamonds, you can pull a diamond at every other pair of vertical ropes or even every third pair.

CHAPTER 8

Glossary

Each term is followed by the number of the page on which it first appears.

alternating hands: a hand-pattern strategy in which right is followed by left and left by right. 59

beats: subdivisions of a pulse. 17

break: a brief phrase that signals the beginning or end of a rhythm, a change in the rhythm, or the entrance or exit of a dancer. 22

cut-time: a way of counting in which there are two pulses to a measure and each pulse is divided into four eighth-note beats. 17

dunduns: double-headed, barrel-shaped bass drums that accompany the djembes in West African rhythms. 46

flam: a double stroke in which both hands play almost simultaneously with equal intensity. 58

four: a pattern is in four if it can be notated on chart with four pulses divided into four beats each. 17

4/4 time: a way of counting in which there are four pulses to a measure and each pulse is divided into four sixteenth notes. 17

4-pulse: four evenly-spaced pulses in a two-measure cycle. 70

ghost notes: barely audible or inaudible touches. 50

Mali weave: a style of weaving ropes to tune a traditional djembe. 85

offbeats: all the beats between pulses except upbeats (on our charts in four that's the ANDS). 48

ONE – the first beat in the first measure of a chart. 22

phrasing: where a repeating part begins and ends. 31

polyrhythm: in simplified terms, the pattern created when two different pulses are played at the same time. 70

pulling a diamond: tightening a traditional djembe by pulling one rope over another. 84

pulse: the underlying metronomic rhythm people feel in their bodies when music is played. 16

six: two measures of **6/8 time**. 62

6/8 time: a way of counting in which there are two pulses to a measure and each pulse is divided into three eighth notes beats. 62

6-pulse: six evenly-spaced pulses in a two-measure cycle. 72

sixteenth notes: two notes played in the space of one eighth note. 81

support drum parts: the repetitive parts that provide the rhythmic foundation for the dancers and the lead drummer. 23

swing feel: When a pattern in four is played with a swing feel, the notes on the ANDS are played slightly later, so they're closer to the numbered beats. 47

12/8 time: a way of counting in which there are four pulses to a measure and each pulse is divided into three eighth notes beats. 62

upbeats: beats that fall exactly midway between pulses. 48

CHAPTER 9

Sources for further study

On the web

Eric Charry's website:
www.wesleyan.edu/~echarry/
jembearticle/article.html

The jembe list FAQ:
http://sherouse.home.
mindspring.com/jembe-listfaq

Djembe and Mande Music Resource
and Reference Page:
www.nauticom.net/users/tcd/
djembemande/index.html

Books and videos on West African drumming and culture

African Rhythm and African
Sensibility by John Chernoff, The
University of Chicago Press, 1979
(book).

Djembefola, Interama, 1991 (documentary video about Mamady Keita).

Mande Music: Traditional and Modern
Music of the Maninka and Mandinka
of Western Africa by Eric Charry, The
University of Chicago Press (book
available summer of 2000).

Instructional books and videos on djembe and dundun playing

African Percussion – The Djembe by
Serge Blanc, 1997 (book with CD).

My Life the the Djembe by Mamady
Keita (book).

The Rhythms of Guinea, West Africa
(Volumes 1 & 2) with Karamba
Diabate, Third Ear Productions
(videos).

Traditional Rhythms of the Mandingue
by Mamady Keita (videos, Vol. 1 for
beginners and Vol. 2 for intermediates).

CDs

Adam Drame (Playasound): Mandingo
Drums Volumes 1 and 2

Famadou Konate (Buda Records):
Malinke Rhythms and Songs

Farafina (RealWorld): Faso Denou and
Bolomakote

Fatala (RealWorld): Gongoma Times

Mamady Keita (Fonti Musicali):
Mogobalu, Wassolon, Afo, and
Nankama

Ensemble National de la Republique
de Guinee (Musique du Monde): Les
Ballets Africains

Les Percussions de Guinee (Buda
Records): Volumes 1 and 2

Articles

Mamady Keita's "Kassa" by Michael
Williams, Percussive Notes Magazine,
April 1997 (transcription of a djembe
solo).

Mamady Keita's "Mendiani" by
Michael Williams, Percussive Notes
Magazine, August 1999 (transcription
of a djembe solo).

1	+	2	+	3	+	4	+	1	+	2	+	3	+	4	+

1	+	2	+	3	+	4	+	1	+	2	+	3	+	4	+

1	+	2	+	3	+	4	+	1	+	2	+	3	+	4	+

1	+	2	+	3	+	4	+	1	+	2	+	3	+	4	+

1	+	2	+	3	+	4	+	1	+	2	+	3	+	4	+

1	2	3	4	5	6	1	2	3	4	5	6

1	2	3	4	5	6	1	2	3	4	5	6

1	2	3	4	5	6	1	2	3	4	5	6

1	2	3	4	5	6	1	2	3	4	5	6

1	2	3	4	5	6	1	2	3	4	5	6

Also available from Dancing Hands Music

$24.95

Conga Drumming
A Beginner's Guide to Playing with Time

BY ALAN DWORSKY AND BETSY SANSBY

This 160-page book with CD is a complete, step-by-step course on conga drumming. It teaches families of drum parts for several authentic Afro-Caribbean rhythms, including rumba, bomba, calypso, conga, and bembe. We use the same simple charting system and friendly teaching style as in HOW TO PLAY DJEMBE. Life-like illustrations show you the proper technique for each stroke. And the CD that's included contains a sample recording of each of the 175 drum parts taught in the book as well examples of how the parts sound together.

"Fantastic!" – RHYTHM MAGAZINE

"There is no other source for this kind of information that is as simply and sensibly explained, and contains such a wealth of rhythms. CONGA DRUMMING welcomes rather than intimidates beginners. Dig into this book and in a very short time you will be playing well. Bravo and muchas gracias Alan and Betsy!"
– DRUM MAGAZINE

"The best book of its kind."
– ARTHUR HULL

Learning to hit the drum using rhythms in four   27

Rhythm 6-4: Bomba low drum part

1	+	2	+	3	+	4	+	1	+	2	+	3	+	4	+
△				O		O	O	△				O	O	O	O
R				L		L	R	R				L	R	L	R

To make the slap, start from the same position that you started from to make the open tone. Pivot your hand upward from the wrist. Then whip your fingers down onto the drumhead while driving your palm down and slightly forward onto the edge of the drum. Cup your hand so that only the pads of the fingertips hit the head. The cup should be slight; you should only be able to slide a pencil between your palm and the drumhead, not a golf ball.

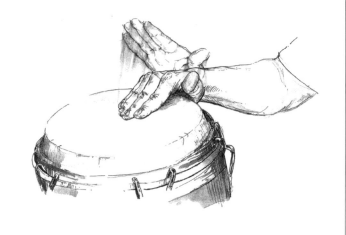

$29.95

Conga Drumming DVD
A Beginner's Video Guide

This DVD brings the book CONGA DRUMMING to life, and gives you a chance to see how all the basic patterns are supposed to be played. It's also a great chance to learn proper playing technique, because we teach each stroke using multiple camera angles and slow-motion photography.

"A <u>must-see</u> for all beginners."
– MICKEY HART

Featuring instruction by renowned percussionist **Jorge Bermudez**

With sizzling solos on congas and bongos by special guest **Raul Rekow** of **Santana**

"**Slammin!** The best video for learning to play congas."
– CHALO EDUARDO, PERCUSSIONIST WITH SERGIO MENDES

$13.95

Jaguar at Half Moon Lake
BY DANCING HANDS

This CD of original music features Indie-award winning Dean Magraw on acoustic guitar and several world percussionists, including Congolese master drummer Coster Massamba on djembe, Jorge Bermudez on bongos, Marc Anderson on talking drum, and Alan Dworsky on congas. You can hear excerpts from JAGUAR on tracks 12–16 of the CD that comes with HOW TO PLAY DJEMBE.

"Luminous"
– NEW MUSIC REVIEW

"Gorgeous melodies and mesmerizing rhythms"
– DIRTY LINEN

Secrets of the Hand
Soloing Strategies for Hand Drummers

BY ALAN DWORSKY AND BETSY SANSBY

This book is for hand drummers who want to play complex solos using simple sequences of hand strokes. Whether you play djembe or conga, the practical hand-pattern strategies explained here will help you get the most out of your hands with the least amount of effort. And whether you want to solo in a traditional African or Afro-Cuban ensemble, in a drum circle, in a band, or in your living room along with your favorite CDs, SECRETS OF THE HAND will help you take your playing to the next level.

$24.95

CD with samples of every pattern in **Secrets of the Hand** now available at dancinghands.com

The Joy of Six for Solo Piano or Keyboard
A Polyrhythmic Journey in 6/8 Time

BY ALAN DWORSKY

In THE JOY OF SIX, Alan Dworsky adapts African and Afro-Cuban polyrhythms to the keyboard in a world-beat classical style. At the heart of the book are four beautiful solo pieces designed to teach different rhythms and rhythmic concepts. Each piece is covered in a separate lesson, where it's broken down into bite-sized patterns that start easy and gradually get more difficult. The CD that comes with the book contains a recording of every pattern and piece, making THE JOY OF SIX a complete self-instruction package.

$24.95

Hear sample audio clips at dancinghands.com

Slap Happy
How to Play World-Beat Rhythms With Just Your Body and a Buddy

BY ALAN DWORSKY AND BETSY SANSBY

SLAP HAPPY is a fun, funky way for kids of all ages to learn about rhythm. We've taken drum rhythms from Africa and the Caribbean (including Kuku and Sunguru Bani from HOW TO PLAY DJEMBE) and turned them into body rhythms you can step, clap, and slap with a buddy. And you can hear how every pattern sounds on the slap-along CD that comes with the book.

$19.95

Learn to Solo on Djembe or Conga
A Step-By-Step Course

BY ALAN DWORSKY

This series is for any djembe player or conga drummer who wants to learn to solo in a systematic way. Each lesson consists of an hour-long CD you can play along with. And each CD comes with a booklet containing charts and explanations of all the patterns you'll be playing.

On the CDs, each pattern is played for about two minutes in four different ways: slowly on djembe, slowly on conga, medium fast on djembe, and medium fast on conga. The djembe tracks are played over West African grooves and the conga tracks are played over Afro-Cuban grooves.

LESSON 1: The Power of Pairs
LESSON 2: The Rippled 8 and the Illusion of Speed
LESSON 3: The Perfect Lick – The Rippled 6
LESSON 4: The Funky Offbeat Path
LESSON 5: Hip Deep in Six
LESSON 6: Getting Off the Grid with Quarter-Note Triplets
LESSON 7: Upbeats and Half-Note Triplets Over a Burning Disco Groove
LESSON 8: Checkered Licks Over a Polyrhythmic Pulse in Six (2 CDs)

Each CD/booklet lesson is $14.95

You can hear sample audio clips at dancinghands.com

"An ingenious method for understanding the mystery of how to solo – hidden from most hand drummers until now!"
– GARY MEITROTT, FOUNDER AND DIRECTOR OF DRUM JOURNEYS OF EARTH

A Rhythmic Vocabulary
A Musician's Guide to Understanding and Improvising with Rhythm

BY ALAN DWORSKY AND BETSY SANSBY

"A goldmine" – DRUM MAGAZINE

If you want to deepen your understanding of rhythm, this 208-page book is for you. It organizes and explains hundreds of African and Afro-Cuban patterns in step-by-step lessons so that you can learn how to create patterns of your own. And it comes with a TIMELINES CD for you to use as a practice partner.

"**The book is masterfully written.** It's like having a good friend sitting next to you, guiding you through each lesson. It explains musical concepts in a way anyone can easily understand. The sections on cross-rhythms and polyrhythms should be required reading for any musician!"
– PROFESSOR MICHAEL WILLIAMS, DEPARTMENT OF MUSIC, WINTHROP UNIVERSITY

DRUM MAGAZINE
Best Percussion Method Book
1999 READERS' POLL

$29.95
CDs with samples of every pattern in
A Rhythmic Vocabulary
now available at dancinghands.com

$14.95

New DVD

How to Play Djembe DVD

WITH ALAN DWORSKY

Now you can see how every pattern in the book HOW TO PLAY DJEMBE is played. This DVD is designed to be used with the book and the audio CD to create a complete learning package: use the book for the charts and explanations, use the CD to hear how every pattern sounds and for play-along practicing, and use the video to see how the hands move on every pattern.

Hip Grooves for Hand Drums
How to Play Funk, Rock & World-Beat Patterns on Any Drum

BY ALAN DWORSKY AND BETSY SANSBY

If you want to play in a band or a church group, or play along with pop, rock, or funk music, this is the book for you. Many of the grooves were adapted from drumset patterns, and all of them sound great even when you're the only drummer on a djembe or a conga drum. HIP GROOVES uses the same easy-to-read charts used in HOW TO PLAY DJEMBE. The CD that comes with the book has samples of every pattern and extended tracks so you can play along. And the optional DVD shows how every pattern in the book is played.

$24.95 Book and CD
$29.95 Book, CD, and DVD!

$19.95 for each DVD

Gentle Djembe for Beginners DVDs

A NEW SERIES WITH ALAN DWORSKY

If you want to play rhythms like the ones in HOW TO PLAY DJEMBE while going easy on your hands, these DVDs are for you.   The patterns have been adapted to include only basses, tones, and touches, so beginners of any age can play safely and comfortably.

Each Gentle Djembe DVD will give you the feel of a private lesson along with the thrill of playing in a group. And you can watch the trailer for each DVD at dancinghands.com.

"The most non-intimidating way for beginning beginners to get started." Arthur Hull, author of "Drum Circle Spirit"

You can call toll-free to order at **1-800-898-8036** or order online at **dancinghands.com**